This book
is dedicated to us —
all of us human beings
who by helping each other
can make our planet
paradise
here and now.

© Planetary Alliance Network, Inc 1995

ISBN 1 899171 95 9

First published in Great Britain in 1995 by

Findhorn Press

The Press Building, The Park
Findhorn, Forres IV36 0TZ, Scotland
01309-690582 / *fax* 690036 /*e-mail* thierry@findhorn.org
url http:/www.gaia.org/findhornpress

Based on talks by Raja

Compiled and edited by the H.E.L.P. team

Typeset by Findhorn Press
Printed and bound in England by J.W. Arrowsmith Ltd., Bristol

British Library cataloguing in publication Data.
A catalogue record for this book is available
from the British Library

Preface

In every age throughout history, humans have recognised their need for help and turned to their wise ones for guidance. Today the need for help is perhaps greater than in any other age. It appears that we need help in every aspect of our lives, and the need is so desperate that we are listening to any and every source of guidance available: UFOs, talking to dolphins, to the dead, and to those with psychic powers. Is there help out there? Is there guidance here? Can anyone help? What can we do? Where are they guiding us?

We have a choice! We can continue to depend on 'the wise' to keep helping us out, or we can learn to help ourselves. We can wait for the messiah to come and build the kingdom of heaven on earth or help each other to create it now!

Help! This very word seems to have become the most popular in human existence, perhaps more popular than Love or God. Why?

At this critical time we have reached a point where we have become aware of our acute need for help — not just individually, but also collectively. Humanity as a whole is confused, even lost and needs help in order to find its direction and balance. Our cry for help implies a crisis which can only be overcome with nothing less than a spirit of co-operation. This is why H.E.L.P. can become the most important channel of love and service for all races around the world.

Clearly we are at a critical threshold of human evolution. There is a new world disorder, and what we need now are the tools for transformation that can help humanity move through this transition with clarity and confidence — to a positive outcome.

We would like to thank you for buying and reading the H.E.L.P Book., a companion to *Panlife — Principles for Personal and Planetary Transformation*. These two volumes together will, we hope, contribute to the practical and spiritual means necessary to take us into the new epoch and beyond.

About the Author

Raja is the originator of the H.E.L.P Programme and the founder of the P.A.N Academy.

Born and raised in Africa, he spent most of his childhood playing in the wilderness, observing the drama of nature. His mother encouraged him in these crucial years to absorb and value these experiences. She died when he was fourteen years of age. Raja then embarked on a voyage of discovery, travelling and working throughout Europe, Africa and Asia.

By the time he was eighteen he had seen, worked and lived with some of the most ancient and complex cultures in the world. Raja was now becoming a man, but a man without roots and in need of a sense of place where he could develop what he called his 'manhood'.

"I had reached a cross-roads where the only choice was either to join a monastery or the Royal Marine Commandos."

He joined the Royal Marines and on passing out was assigned to the Mountain and Arctic Commando and then to Reconnaissance Troop based in Scotland.

Nicknamed 'The Monk', he lived like a monk and soon excelled to become a soldier in the Special Forces. Throughout his work in the armed forces, he did what he said and completed tasks because life depended on it. It was in the armed forces that he learned how to master the physical world and combine it with his spiritual ideals. He resigned in order to begin his life's work.

"I hope the world at large can utilise the extraordinary potential of this man."

J.D. Wassall. M.B.E., M.M.
(Corps Regimental Sergeant Major).

At present Raja instructs at the P.A.N Academy which trains social and global pioneers. He is a rare combination of a practical and spiritual man. Truly one of the quiet leaders of our time.

Contents

Overview

The Discovery of H.E.L.P.

I was born and raised on the outskirts of Dar-es-salaam, (which means 'a haven for peace'), on the coast of Tanzania in Africa.

I spent most of my infant days playing in the wilderness. My mother encouraged me to absorb these experiences, often telling me stories from different races and religions.

She died when I was fourteen, and this led me to embark on a journey of discovery. Living a nomadic way, I wandered from country to country seeing all kinds of weird and wonderful places. I met many wise people and had mystical experiences. Yet, I felt alone and isolated in a world where no one cared for me. What I really wanted to discover was love and a way to help myself.

In order to 'survive', I became ruthless — to take care of number one. Cocooning myself inside a loveless world led me on a downward spiral of desperation . . . The day came when I cried out "help me!" from the very core of my being. As I sat helpless, I realised that there was only one person that was going to help me. My-Self! Asking myself for help was the turning point. Talking with myself was the channel to my Divine Being — the source of love and life. My Divine Being led me to the discovery of the H.E.L.P. Pathways.

I know what it feels like to be helpless. I was fortunate enough to find these skills and now I wish to share them. H.E.L.P. is an extension of my life. It provides simple skills that can be used by all individuals enabling them to help themselves in the most difficult of situations.

H.E.L.P. is a way to love and live. It is based on universal skills that procreate life. Once you become familiar with these skills you are then *free* — to do as you will. Life is easy if you know how to live it.

To help is to love, to love is to live.

Each one of us is capable of helping ourselves and each other, and that's the way we shall create a living paradise on earth.

Bharut Raja

Background

The earth is the mother of our species and all of our fellow travellers: the family of living creatures. Four-and-a-half billion years ago the earth was formed, and perhaps half a billion years ago the first signs of life arose on the planet. Over the next 1.5 billion years, life evolved steadily into more complex, diverse and adaptable creatures until around a million years ago when it produced the initial species of mankind, the most complex and ingenious species of them all. Imagine the earth's existence to date has been a year long; civilisation emerged less than a minute ago! To the marvels of evolution we humans have been able to add our own skills such as art, science and technology, social organisation and spirituality.

As our attainments became ever more diverse, the evolutionary foundation beneath our feet became more and more shaky. Now, in spite of all we have learned and achieved, or rather because of it, we hold the entire world hostage to 'ecocide', and with our irresponsible actions we threaten every living thing on our planet including each other. It is when we consider the global scale of humanity's influence within the biosphere that we can really appreciate the mighty task before us. In essence it is to transform humanity's relationship with the earth, from one that is harmful and destructive to one of responsible, creative stewardship.

Preachers, teachers, leaders and people of goodwill please help each other! The future depends on you — on us. The will to act and cooperate must be found within each individual. Ultimately, a healthy environment will only manifest when a sufficient number of men and women demand it through their collective will. When action is taken with good intent, the outcome is always positive. It is therefore the minds and hearts of people that must change. Whatever we do to the earth, we do to ourselves. Acid rain falls on people, not just on fir trees.

We abuse the planet just as we abuse each other and abuse ourselves. The earth is dying. It is dying because it is being raped, by humans who are raping and killing each other too.

The problem is not a lack of spirituality or goodwill, but a crisis of evolution. This may sound like a contradiction, yet as I think about human evolution, I feel that we have come a very long way. It is true that we still have wars, hunger, torture, violence, child abuse and rape. Those things have always (at least in recorded history) been a part of humanity. However, what I feel is very different now is that those things are becoming unacceptable. It was only a short time ago in our history when it was acceptable for a man to beat his wife and children; not that long ago since slavery was acceptable, and only very recently that rape has been seen as not only unacceptable, but also not the fault of the woman.

History is full of horrors and it is only very recently that these horrors have been questioned and things have really changed. I do not believe that we live in a more violent society than in the past — I believe that we are entering an age which is much more at peace and ease.

The 'crisis', if we can call it that, is in our consciousness — we are becoming aware of our past, present and future. The crisis we face today is composed of the problems which have existed for thousands of years. The resistance to changing from the old way to the new way is what is causing the crisis.

To learn from the present crisis and build a solid foundation for generations to come, we need to find practical, workable solutions for today's problems. Time and time again we have heard people talk of paradigm shifts. Currently there is confusion over the number of paradigms with very little, if any, practical help as to what we should do to save each other and our planet from extinction.

We know in our hearts what we do wrong. We hear from the wise what is right, but no one tells us, simply and clearly, how to put things right in practical terms.

The way of H.E.L.P. attempts to do just that. We begin by acknowledging the condition of the earth and what or who has been responsible for the problems we face today.

The New Epoch

To cut a long story short, there is a new world disorder. The irony is that despite all our scientific, academic and spiritual knowledge, we have a crisis on our hands. Why? What is the cause of this crisis? When we ask the experts, they all give us a different explanation. Has our species made a mess of the earth as part of our learning process, or have we deliberately set out to destroy ourselves and the earth? Is our species about to end its life span or enter a new era of evolution?

If you look at the human species from an evolutionary perspective, humanity as it stands today is in its infancy and as such we have made a mess on the planet. The time has come to clean up the mess — grow up and enter the next phase of our evolutionary journey. On the basis of this understanding, all our problems can be seen and solved as a part of one crisis - the crisis in human evolution.

> The crisis is evolution.
> The solution is evolution.
> The challenge is to help our species evolve.

Looking back at the origin of our species, it seems that we have been getting ready for some time to take a quantum leap. Although we can draw on some knowledge from the past, the leap we are about to take is going to separate us from the animal kingdom once and for all. In essence, we are going to become a new species whose consciousness is not grounded in survival and extinction, i. e. hunter—hunted, but in love, compassion and co-operation, i. e. helper—helped.

We are reaching a critical mass in the number of individuals participating in a new wave of consciousness based on the idea of help. Helping each other is going to be the touchstone which will enable humans to evolve into what I call *Pan human* (Pan meaning 'one complete whole'). During the coming epoch, humans will disappear and a new kind of creature — Pan human — will come into being. Their perception of life will not be based on fear and illusion but on consciousness and reality. As we move from illusion to reality, the duality that separates us will become unity.

Pan humans will perceive the world as one. Matter and spirit, male and female, good and evil will all be embraced by the consciousness that all-is-one: this is the nature of the universe referred to as Pantheism (pantheism — identification of God with the universe). All the conflict in our past and present will disappear as each one of us begins to see life is this way.

The solution to human evolution and global transformation is to help each individual develop his or her foundations of living and the skills necessary to maintain health and help each other. As each one of us acts according to the new consciousness based on co-operation, we send ripples into the world. Even the smallest action of help will directly or indirectly affect every other creature now and in the future. To help is to love, and love will be the motivating factor in the coming epoch.

We are living at a most precious moment in the universe, as we consciously choose to enter a new epoch. Each one of us is knowingly or unknowingly involved in the greatest crisis since our species began to emerge from the animal kingdom. We are at the dawn of the creation of a new kind of creature. We are the first creatures to become aware of our awesome capacity to envision our future and create it. The future looks bright and beautiful as we see the world with love. The new world is at hand — in your hands. The outcome is entirely up to us.

You and Me.

> *"Let us come together and see what kind of*
> *a world we can create for our children."*

Sitting Bull

Competition to Co-operation

As humanity moves into a new era, more and more people are moving from competition to cooperation as a means of providing a life-support system.

It is not by chance that you have picked up this book! As you put the information and insights gained from this book into practice you too are becoming a part of a new era — a new breed of human being. In choosing to read this book, you have in fact affirmed your willingness to change from a competitive (hunter—hunted) to a co-operative (helper—helped) approach towards relating with the outside world.

This process may take several years to complete on an individual level and will most definitely be no less challenging than climbing Everest without oxygen. In moving from competition to co-operation you may encounter resistance not only from within yourself, but also from your family, friends and colleagues. Why? In choosing to trade in competition (win—loose) for co-operation (win—win) you are not only going against the current flow of society, but also reversing and redirecting the psyche of humanity into the unknown. Going into the unknown, even if it is for the better and sometimes because it is for the better, brings all kinds of fears and phobias to the fore. For millions of years, the human psyche has relied on competition as a means for survival, which it will not let go of easily.

Only understanding of the need to change and the way to do it will promote the transition. Whilst competition has been necessary so far in our evolution, we have now created an environment where co-operation is becoming the means for survival. Over the past hundred thousand years, we have learned to couple intelligence with competition. We have in fact mastered the art of competition to the nth degree, and control our total environment, where winners get all and losers get nothing. This process is wiping out thirty-five species of life every month, killing over one-hundred and twenty million people of starvation a year and making two hundred million people homeless. Humanity is at war with itself and the earth. War is the ultimate manifestation of competition. Surely, they will tell you, competition is healthy. Is it really?

Firstly, competition by it very nature results in the haves and the have-nots — in this scenario the difference is life and death. This brutal conflict can only continue for so long until there is anarchy. The threat of atomic war may be over, but anarchy on an unprecedented level is a real possibility, unless each one of us makes the transition from competition to cooperation.

Secondly, as more and more individuals make the transition, there also exists the possibility of a violent reaction from the status quo, all be it delivered by 'the hidden hand'. Co-operation by its very nature results in a more equal distribution of land, wealth, resources and power. Those who have come to control so much of our current world culture have done so by mastering the art of war (competition), passed on from generation to generation. In the past, these people have been dislodged from their position by means of revolution. The drawback with revolution is that the poor always remain poor regardless of the change in power.

Our aim is not revolution, but evolution. By becoming aware of the need for transition from competition to co-operation, we shall avert anarchy, war and revolution. Even those in power now will see the sense in this. This is not to say that there will be no reaction or resistance as we move from the old to the new. However, because evolution is slower and often unseen it will provoke less direct conflict. Less resistance will make the transition more manageable, smoother and faster. The secret of social change is to initiate changes slowly and quietly without an axe to grind.

"He, who has an axe to grind, has an axe."

As you apply the content of this book, be aware that you are in fact becoming a pioneer of social change — a new breed of human being. As such you may unknowingly provoke those around you. I suggest that in the early stages of your transition you stay away from the sceptics and the cynics. Instead, seek like-minded people who will help you adapt to the new way.

How to use this book

This book is dedicated to all those who are in need of help. As such, all the content is designed primarily for individuals who feel the need for change in their lives. Although the book can be dipped into at any page, I suggest you start at the beginning at least for the first time round. I also suggest you read slowly, stopping for breath to reflect on the insight you have gained. One insight is often enough to change your current situation, or even your whole life.

Pace and Flow

As you get into the book, you may find the need to alter your lifestyle, such as spending more time in silence; living alone or together; stopping work or starting work or maybe ending certain relationships or starting new ones. At first you may feel overwhelmed by the sheer number of changes you need to make. Coming to terms with how you have lived and what you need to do can lead to a state of shock! This is natural. Allow all this to happen and trust in the flow. Find your own pace. If you catch yourself trying to control your life, take a deep breath, hold for a second or two and then release with a sigh of relief.

Making Changes

After you read each part, make a plan for change. This process is vital for you to help yourself. Making changes can be easy or difficult depending on your past and present circumstances. There are many obstacles that can prevent us from changing our current situation, but most, if not all of them, can be overcome by a simple process called active learning or active living.

Each chapter begins with twenty statements to stimulate the imagination. At the end of each chapter you can explore the significance of the skill and work with the formula for making changes. As you read each page, make a mental note or mark points of interest. Then use the insight gained to find solutions and actions to promote change.

Who needs H.E.L.P.?

Today there are over five billion human beings living on the earth, each one of us trying to eke out a living on some level or another. By the year 2040 the human population may have doubled to ten billion. Most of us will be alive but what kind of life will we have? Common sense tells us that the quality of our present living conditions will be halved in all areas. This may be acceptable to some, but for those who are already on the breadline it spells certain death unless they can fulfil their basic needs.

Each one of us needs help to make it through daily life, hence the lyric *"I'll get by with a little help from my friends"*. Yet the kind of help we need varies from person to person around the world. Wherever we may be living on the earth each one of us needs help in our unique situation. Some need help with medical care, housing, education or simply to eat. Others may need legal advice, therapy for addictions, sexual problems, insomnia or simply a hug after a hard day. Just as there are infinite needs for help, there are endless ways we can get help and give it. The question is: if there are so many ways of helping ourselves and each other, why are so many people still suffering in the world? With so many channels of helping and healing available to us, why is humanity not at peace and living in a state of paradise?

Millions of people and animals are suffering on the earth now. Yet, we can't help them. Why?

Is it possible that help is always at hand, but we simply don't know how to get or to give it? The world is moving so fast, individuals have lost focus of what is really important in their lives. We have lost touch with ourselves and become isolated within the mass of civilisation. Separated from ourselves, we separate from each other and the earth. We end up living lonely and empty lives, unable to ask for help, not knowing how to get it or give it to those in need. Is it any wonder why the word help is so often used, yet what does the word 'help' mean, and what purpose does it serve?

Our first cry for help was when we were babies in need of milk and safety. Our subsequent cries come when we reach points in our lives where we cannot get what we need to move forward. The struggle then continues until, and unless, we solve the problem and fulfil the need. To do this we must first be aware of what the need is. Far too often, we do and ask for something which we have come to rely on or accept as a natural part of our daily lives. In reality these are often superficial or unreal needs, and when they are met they do not fulfil us on a deeper level. We must get in touch with our primal needs and learn to fulfil them ourselves. As Gandhi once said, *"There is enough in this world for everyone's need; there is not enough for everyone's greed"*.

When our basic needs are being met then our creativity, which comes from our inner voice, can flow. To fulfil these basic needs we must go out into the world and form relationships with other people, animals and the earth.

The Co-operative Paradigm

So far in the history of humanity, relationships have meant competition between individuals and nations to assure their future against scarcity of resources. Hence we have a world of haves and have-nots. When we help each other to fulfil our individual needs, competition is replaced by co-operation. The word 'help' implies a spirit of co-operation, and the more we co-operate, the more creative and comfortable we all become.

> *"In numberless animal societies,*
> *the struggle between separate individuals*
> *for the means of existence disappears;*
> *struggle is replaced by co-operation."*
>
> Charles Darwin.

The new paradigm for the next millennium reiterates that we must make this move from competition to co-operation. The question is: HOW?

The Co-operative Aim

The aim is to replace competition with co-operation. The question is, how do we assist the individual to make this transition and not lose out? It is clear that each one of us must learn to co-operate — to help each other. What is lacking is a practical, workable process which can be used by everyone around the world to make this transformation. The H.E.L.P. process fulfils this need and is the bridge which will take us from competition to co-operation.

The World Starts with Myself

The way forward is for each one of us to learn how to first help ourselves and then each other. No matter what kind of help we may need at a particular age or stage in life, we can use these elements to help ourselves and move on. Once we have learned how to help ourselves, we can help others — by showing them how they can help themselves, and by being a living example of the co-operative paradigm.

It may be useful in quiet times for you to sit and reflect on the idea that "The world starts with myself". It is a revelation to find that to heal the world, we must start by healing ourselves.

Extinction or Evolution

The time has come for humanity to take an evolutionary leap into the new epoch. The question is, *how?* Many individuals want to help create a better world but feel unable, alone and helpless. This book shows us how: by using a simple, unique process of human evolution that is helping individuals, around the world to help each other and the earth.

The purpose of this book is to take H.E.L.P. into the hearts and homes of the people. That is all of us, you and me.

Pathways to H.E.L.P.

Active Living

H.E.L.P. is based on active living. This means that we live to learn and learn to act. This process is called life experience. Learning by experience is the most powerful form of learning. It is how we learned to walk, sing, play musical instruments, roller-skate, swim, add up, value and form opinions. All these learning experiences are based on an instinctual learning process used by all living things. We can use this process consciously to help ourselves evolve and learn new and exciting ways of living.

You can use this process right now. Did you know that most people breathe at one-fifth of their capacity? Now you know, try this: sit up and take a deep breath, filling your lungs fully. Hold for a second or two and exhale freely. Do that again four times. How do you feel? If you feel good, then adapt your daily life to include this practice.

In the same way, you can use the active living process to adopt new ways in your lifestyle. Once you have learnt how to apply the process, you will use it instinctively — like riding a bicycle!

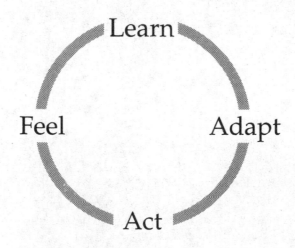

Learn

Feel   Adapt

Act

1. Learn

The whole aim in life is to learn lessons and to move on. If we don't learn, then we keep repeating the lesson until we do so.

- Learn about yourself and your goal.
- Identify the problems and the solutions attempted so far.
- Discuss the possible solutions and get feedback/information.

Learn to use what you already know and that way, you will learn what you really need to know.

2. Adapt

Life is never exactly the way we want it to be. Our lives are constantly changing and we must change with change constantly.

- Contemplate on the specific areas of development. Contemplation is a simple process of sitting quietly and reflecting on a topic, action or situation.
- Develop a clear definition of the change to be achieved.
- Make a game plan for action, with clear, simple steps.

Adapting new patterns of thought and behaviour can be very challenging. You will need to let go of the old for the new.

3. Act

Action is a vital ingredient in the learning process. Getting into or out of trouble will almost always mean going into the unknown!

- Visualise and play act the actual change process exactly, by yourself or with a group.
- Develop a personal support network for moral, practical and spiritual support.
- Implement the change strategy with total commitment. Trust the process.

As you act on a new idea or thought, you will begin a process of renewal which will affect your body, emotions and mind. Every physical action directly alters your total condition.

4. Feel

The modern world has produced generations who are out of touch with their feelings and emotions. When we allow ourselves to experience fully, we realise that what is missing in our lives is the total experience.

Many of us learn to anaesthetise our feelings; how often have we heard the saying "grin and bear it"? Experiencing fully means being free to access and express feelings you may have kept locked away for years. This takes some getting used to: it is part of accepting who you are.

- Feel what you are going through, laugh, cry, be quiet, etc.

- Listen to your intuition before you start new cycles of experiences. Celebrate whether you 'fail' or 'succeed'. All life is about learning lessons. If we celebrate only when we succeed, more than half our lives will be spent in misery!

- Avoid 'beating yourself up' for not achieving instant, total success. If it's difficult, it's not because you are weak or a failure, but because change is challenging and most of us need help and support to increase our strength for the task.

Lastly, you must decide how much change you need in your lifestyle. For some of you only minor changes will be necessary, others may need a transformation in depth. Both minor and major changes take time. Sometimes it takes longer to change a minor habit than to change a major pattern of addiction. Faith, patience and perseverance will be needed. If you find yourself alone, speak to someone, go to support groups or organise one at your home.

The H.E.L.P. Process

Helping ourselves and each other is a natural part of our lives, as natural as breathing, playing, crying or laughing. From the day we are born to the day we are buried is one continuous journey of learning to help ourselves and each other. One's cry for help is a chance for another to help and grow. The refusal to help someone in need is a denial to acknowledge and ask for help — it is a denial to live and learn new ways of working together. The moment we stop asking for help is the moment life's powerful forces are cut off. This is why it says in the Bible: *"ask and you shall receive; knock and the door will be opened; seek and you shall find"*. The H.E.L.P. Pathways present the skills needed to put this simple truth into practice.

H.E.L.P. is not another philosophy or paradigm. It is a practical, workable process which can be understood and used by every individual right now. Try it!

You can use the H.E.L.P. process as your life-support system to improve your health, home, family and work-life. H.E.L.P. touches all aspects of our lives. It can be used in all facets of society — in education, services, business and organisations.

The diagram opposite shows the foundations and skills which are central to being human. Most people tend to neglect, rather than improve these foundations and skills for living. Why? The first reason is misplaced priorities. We tend to think that whilst we focus on our professions and careers our life-support system will somehow take care of itself. The second is an evolutionary blindspot, passed on from generation to generation. Throughout human evolution the demands made on an individual by their society and surroundings have changed drastically. Yet the life-support system of a human being has been systematically eroded under the 'march of progress'. Human beings, like other creatures have very basic and primal needs which must be met if we are to live creative, fulfilled lives.

During years of working with people from diverse backgrounds I have come in contact with many individuals who have

Foundations

Home:

A place where we can rest and recover.

Health:

A state of total well-being.

Family:

A sense of kinship with family and friends.

Work:

A livelihood which is meaningful.

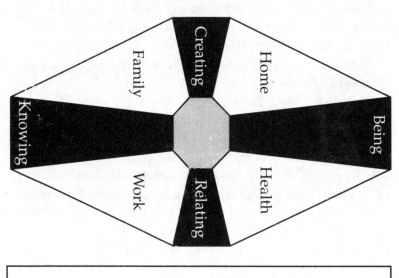

Skills

Relating:

With oneself, other people and nature.

Creating:

Any thought, emotion or action.

Knowing:

To know things. To know that you know.

Being:

A state of peace and ease.

accomplished an incredible degree of outward success and yet found themselves struggling with an inner hunger, a deep need for *self-nurturance*. The reality, of course, is that the more you nurture yourself, the more creative and comfortable you become in all areas of your life. A brief glance at the diagram opposite will reveal how much we are actually conditioned to ignore our real life needs. The H.E.L.P. process presents an integrated system of living. Anyone, anywhere can use it with very little cost and create a life worth living.

- The first step is to ask yourselves honestly, which of the four foundations, i.e. home, health, family and work need developing.
- The second step is to simply focus on your basic needs and trust that everything else will fall into place.
- The third step is to develop the skills of knowing, relating, creating and being, which are necessary to establish these foundations.

Knowing

We begin with knowing because it is here that we learn skills such as honesty. It is through the door of honesty that we can accept our limitations and begin to learn how to gain access to new knowledge. For example, even becoming aware that there existed ways of knowing new things led to major changes in my life. This is the key to individual transformation. Over ninety percent of our thought patterns are the same from day to day and that's why we often suffer and feel stuck. Hence, if we are to become truly unlimited human beings, we have to develop insight into our limitations. If I don't know where I am, how can I get where I want to go?

Relating

In order to learn new ways, we need to relate with those who can show them to us. Relating is a skill we used to find our mother's nipple, the first embrace, smile, etc. The way we relate to other people, animals and the earth was learned from our family, friends and society. We are relating to our surroundings all the time — with the elements, colour, texture, form and so on. Indeed, every time we relate to something or someone, we create a thought, feeling, form or product. Relating is the art of doing and whatever we have been doing in the past has shaped our reality today. This means that whatever you want to 'do' in the future, you will need relationships to accomplish it.

Creating

Creating what you want, be it an ideal home, perfect health, an invention or vision, is a matter of skill. Many people have visions and dreams, but are unable to manifest them. They simply lack the skill and know-how necessary to go from idea to completion. When you have learned how to apply the skills of creating, you can then apply that know-how to creating whatever your heart desires. For example Leonardo da Vinci invented the parachute, the flying machine, the drill press, the odometer, the helicopter, the military tank, and painted the Mona Lisa. It is possible that he may have unknowingly used the principle of creating to be productive but because he neglected the foundations of living (home, health, relationships) his personal life was far from fulfilled.

Being

We all want to live in a state of well-being. The term well-being is used in almost every health magazine, therapy and seminar. The question is, how do we use all this information, these therapies and techniques to bring about well-being? The H.E.L.P. process will enable you to receive, give or gain access to whatever it is you need to bring about total well-being. This how it works. When we relate with each other, animals and the earth, it gives rise to the desire to create. What we learn from the interplay between relating and creating results in knowing. We then make choices based on what we know and act on them. This in turn determines the quality of our being. Life is how you make it!

The H.E.L.P. Choice Process

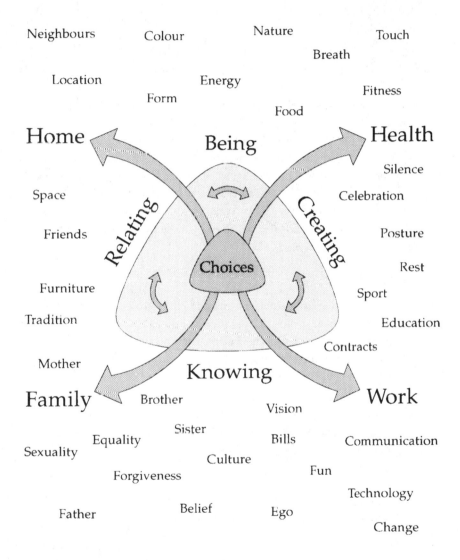

Neighbours   Colour   Nature   Touch

Breath

Location   Energy   Fitness

Form

Food

Home   Being   Health

Silence

Space   Relating   Creating   Celebration

Friends   Posture

Choices   Rest

Furniture   Sport

Tradition   Education

Contracts

Mother   Knowing

Family   Work

Brother   Vision

Sister   Bills   Communication

Equality

Sexuality   Culture

Forgiveness   Fun

Technology

Father   Belief   Ego

Change

The Practise Of H.E.L.P.

Everyday you make thousands of choices which affect your health, home, family and work. If you are not happy, the chances are that you have made the wrong choices. You can change that simply by making the right choices. To get started I suggest you ask yourself two simple questions:

1) What is the best way for me to live?

2) What is the best thing for me to seek?

By applying the H.E.L.P. process, you will connect with what I call your Divine Being. Your Divine Being has the perfect idea of your ideal state. Most people are far from living in an ideal. Although they have flashes of what that may be, because of ignorance, they fail to connect with its source. Instead, they have contrary pictures of disease, death and destruction stamped in the subconcious. If we are to live in peace and ease, we need to reconnect with our Divine Being and make new choices on individual and collective levels.

Individual

As soon as you start using the H.E.L.P. process, you will be showered with new ideas and new images. Your life and environment will change for the better, for you are guided by your Divine Being where there is a spiritual prototype of your 'ideal condition' — your perfect state of existence.

Many people try to change their circumstances by controlling other people and external events. The only person who need change is yourself. As you make the right choices, all conditions in your life will change for the better. For example, did you choose your clothes today? Are you at ease?

Look back in your life and see how you have attracted either happiness or disaster through your choices.

What is true of a little choice is true of a big choice. When you are living in a state of peace and ease, wherever you go, you take that condition with you. That is personal paradise.

Collective

If you look at the earth as one living being, then you and I are a part of one family — humanity. You are important, as what happens to you and what you do sends ripples around the world.

The world starts with myself.

By using the H.E.L.P. process, you will effortlessly improve the quality of your own life and the state of the earth! How? Just as each one of us chooses to create our personal condition, our choices affect our family, community and country and humanity as a whole. The condition of the earth and humanity is the result of choices made by individuals like you and me. There is a simple equation which each family member, worker and citizen needs to understand.

CHOICE = CONDITION.

At this moment, billions of choices are being made and communicated via words, deeds, radio, TV, images, Internet . . . Yet, the 'condition' is poor because, the choice process is poor. The H.E.L.P. process shows how we can change the suffering and destruction on the earth simply by making the right choices ourselves. That is planetary paradise.

YOU HAVE THE POWER OF CHOICE.

Pan Paradise

From deep within the psyche of humanity has arisen the H.E.L.P. Pathways. The purpose of these pathways is to help create a world living in peace and ease-paradise. The notion of actually creating paradise may seem far-fetched so I ask you to bear with me while I explain what I mean by paradise and the way we can create paradise on earth.

Paradise to me means a state of peace and ease — both of which can be created simply by developing one's foundations of living. For example, the roots of a tree determine its condition. Just as a forest is made up of individual trees, each one of us makes up what we call humanity. Like any other living creature we too have primal needs which must be fulfilled. Although there are many needs, and just as many ways to fulfil them, they can all be reduced to four foundations and four skills of living. By simply nurturing our foundations of living daily we become happy, healthy individuals. In doing so we realign our dis-ease to ease. Ease is the precondition to peace-paradise.

The idea of Paradise, Shangri-La, Eden, etc., has always existed in the psyche of humanity. Just as an acorn contains the secrets of the forest, each one of us knows the idea of paradise. For example, unless a child has been conditioned otherwise, it sees the world as paradise — a place of wonder and miracles. As Jesus put it, *"to enter the kingdom you must become childlike"*. The first step is to make life into a game and have fun! The second is to view the world with the eyes of a child. And the third is to believe that paradise is possible. When we were children, life was paradise, a game which was fun. When the grown-ups did not understand, we built our own little paradise — a den, a tent, a tree house, etc.

In the same way, although our current society does not understand the need for paradise, we owe it to ourselves to create it. This does not mean that we cocoon ourselves in some corner of the world within walls and fences. We have to understand that the door to our home is the door which leads to paradise.

Most people have difficulty in believing that they have the power to create paradise, because they have been weakened by disbelief. Disbelief leads to self-doubt, denying ourselves that which is ours by divine right. *"Everything the kingdom can afford is yours."* Yet, how many people do you know who can say *"my life is paradise"*? Disbelief can be controlled and camouflaged by the use of mind control, but it will always deny you paradise. For example, a lot of people may meditate and attain peace, but the moment they stop it is gone. Others look at paradise as an ideal. The problem with an ideal is that it is always unreachable. What use is meditative bliss or ideals when one's home, health, family and work are in poor condition?

The idea of paradise is ancient, but has it become an ideal because we don't know how to create it? Has our inability led to disbelief and vice-versa? Two thousand years have passed since Jesus said, *"I have come to build the kingdom of heaven on earth"*. Are we are still waiting for the messiah to come and build it for us or can we create paradise ourselves? If Jesus came to build the kingdom of heaven on earth, how would he build it? I believe that the way to create a personal paradise is by tending to one's own foundations of living.

You can begin to create your paradise wherever you are now.

The time has come for us to create *Pan Paradise* on earth. The question is, *how*? So far, our species has mainly used physical activity to create our whole world-culture. Yet, nine tenths of our minds lay dormant! Too much physical activity is destroying the body of humanity and of the earth. We need to open our minds and discover new methods of changing our current conditions and creating new realities.

I am going to introduce you to what I call the *Panlife** process of manifesting the metaphysical into the physical. The following may at first appear unusable; but it will become a stepping stone that will take humanity to paradise. I suggest you try the process for yourself.

* *Panlife* process taken from the Panlife teachings by Raja

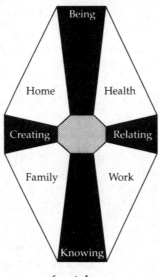

front door

1. Take a good look at the diagram above, and imagine creating your ideal foundations and skills of living.

2. Now close your eyes and take several deep breaths.

3. For each of the foundations of living — Health, Home, Family and Work — choose a symbolic object. For example, for Home, you could have a plaque reading *"home sweet home"*.

4. Then choose a symbolic object for each of the four skills of Knowing, Relating, Creating and Being. For example, you could choose a crystal for Knowing.

5. Close your eyes again and mentally visualise yourself placing these symbolic objects in and around your home according to the layout of the diagram, starting with Knowing at the 'front door' — which signifies the gateway to paradise.

6. Then gather these symbolic objects and physically place them around your home — according to the diagram.

7. Sit quietly each day and concentrate; contemplate what you want each object to manifest in that aspect of your life.

How does it work? Symbols are a method of touching your inner reality. Like touchstones, they are highly charged objects which activate the law of attraction. A symbol is a point of unity between your inner and outer world. The placement of symbolic objects and images connects the subconscious with the outside world. A symbolic object is charged with thoughts and emotions. Symbolic objects and images become activated by strong thoughts and emotions which then manifest as physical objects, conditions or events in your life. When thoughts or emotions reach a certain intensity, they become magnetic and attract to the given space whatever you are focusing on.

Be aware that the symbols and images you connect with will be *manifested* in you life. By contemplating on specific images related to your home, etc, you bring to the forefront of your mind that which will become physical form. In ancient time, our species used stones and carvings to initiate this law of creation. Once the symbolic objects and images are placed, 'the force' remains activated until it is manifest or consciously changed.

The energy must be activated with great intensity-contemplation, otherwise it will fade and become dormant. The intensity of your thoughts and emotions on the symbolic objects and images is vital in the process of physical materialisation.

For example, if you place money in the space of work, then money will be the result of your work.

When you have materialized the symbol in the physical form, it will vanish from your desire. This process will continue again and again until there is a void. It may seem that without symbols you would be a non-being, but this is natural as we exist in a symbolic object — the body.

By playing with symbols, you are changing your inner and outer environment. The nature of symbols therefore can serve as an indication not only of your environment, but your state of consciousness within it. Even the same symbol at varying stages of consciousness will appear differently. The meaning of a symbol will change, therefore, as your consciouness becomes multidimentional.

Take a look around your home and you will see how much the physical (material) and the metaphysical (spiritual) are linked. Take a close look at your front door, at where you cook and eat, sleep and bath; then see how the objects and images you have affect your home, health, family and work, i.e., your life is a reflection of objects and images you love.

Our home is the reflection of the self

When we see the earth as our home and humanity as the occupant, what do we see? Go to any city and you will see symbolic objects and images which its culture is focusing on. Then as you look closely, you will observe its effect on the people. We live in a world where people worship *form* at the cost of neglecting the *formless*. The current world culture is focusing on building bigger, higher, faster, i.e. on great achievements. Behind most great achievements, there are often feelings of fear and insecurity. People who are happy-fulfilled, do not need to prove themselves. They simply live and let live. They just know what they need and what they don't. How much of what we have in our homes, streets, schools, and churches do we really need to be happy? The reason our culture is falling apart like a house of cards is that we are neglecting the very foundations of our lives for the sake of more, material objects and money.

The symbolic objects and images you have chosen reveal to you what is your focus in life —how you have come to be in the position you are in now. This is your big opportunity, for the gates of paradise await you. Be strong and fear not. Let go of all that you do not need, for it is stopping you from entering paradise. Have faith, and focus *only* on tending your foundations of living and behold you shall witness a personal paradise. Your personal paradise can then extend to your family, community, country and on ever expanding levels.

A whole book could be written on the power of symbology. In the next few thousand years, the means of materialising our desires will merge symbology with technology. My aim here is to introduce you to the power of symbology and the means to activate its use. The purpose of this explanation is to re-instate the belief that you have the power to create anything imaginable — including paradise.

Four Universal Skills

The four skills of human evolution, are also the universal mediators of evolution. By evolution, I also mean the development of consciousness. The four skills of knowing, relating, creating and being intersect all realities. These are not only skills, but also channels through which energy flows from one object-identity to another. They are like invisible pathways which connect one reality to another and make creation-evolution continuous. Without these skills (channels), evolution and creation would not exist.

Our space is filled with these channels now and I will explain how their interaction creates new realities on every level of co-existence. At the moment you are participating in the interaction of the energy, atoms, microbes and elements that surround you. By *relating* to each other, we are now *creating* new forms of *knowing* — consciousness. This means that even a stone has consciousness. This is how everything comes into *being*. Of course, this explanation is highly simplified for this is not the time to delve into the mechanics behind this process. However scientists, alchemists, astrologists, artists and craftsmen will know the significance of this process in their relative fields.

What I do want to relay to you is the application of these skills via examples and demonstration. Choose any activity, event or condition and write it clearly in the middle of the triangle.

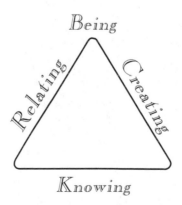

Since the nature of these skills is universal, this can be any activity or aim you have completed. Use your freedom, for it matters not whether you choose the form or the formless. My purpose is to demonstrate that this process governs any reality or realm of existence you choose.

Now do your utmost to cancel out any one or more of the skills that were not present in the process of creating or comprehending the event, activity or condition. Also try to add any skills which you may deem necessary to the process.

Again, this is very simplified, but even subatomic particles which emanate from ' nothingness' obey the same process as they come into being. In the same way you and I came into being via this process. Our parents knew how to relate via intercourse and created a new human being. Energy travelled from one person-identity to another via the interaction of these skills and new life was procreated.

I want you to look at the H.E.L.P. triangle as an oracle; then perharps you can learn the many ways it can be used.

When you want to develop a situation or manifest something new, make a new triangle and write the aim within it. Then contemplate and consciously use the four universal skills daily. The four universal skills contained in The H.E.L.P. Book will enable you to evolve and create any reality you wish.

The Way of
Knowing

How well does each statement describe your pattern of thought and action?

- *I know how to live and what to seek.*
- *I know what my real needs are.*
- *I know that as I fulfil my own needs I become more happy and healthy.*
- *I use every adversity as an opportunity for prosperity.*
- *I know how to find solutions to seemingly impossible problems.*
- *I know how to gain access to new knowledge from inside myself.*
- *Whereas I used to get stuck with my own and other people's patterns of behaviour, now I glide effortlessly.*
- *I am free of addictions and attachments and can show others how to become so.*
- *I have infinite patience and know how to use it everyday.*
- *I have plenty of time to do the things I love and need to do.*
- *I know what it means to be the custodian of the earth and the keeper of the knowledge contained in the wilderness.*
- *I have explored my sexuality to the point of ecstasy, based on love.*
- *I know how to handle the thousands of mystical experiences which exist beyond the realm of rational explanation.*
- *I am fully aware of the effects of the news on my own psyche and that of humanity.*
- *I know how to dissolve resistance within and without myself.*
- *I am completely honest and therefore a force of nature.*
- *I know how to wield absolute power.*
- *I know that all of the suffering in the world is caused by the denial of my own soul.*
- *I know what is true for me is true for all.*
- *I am the master of my own destiny — my life is paradise.*

Introduction

Are you living or surviving? Is your life a battleground, on the inside and the outside, between survival, security, sex and sensation? Do you have a need in any area of your life? What is that need and where did it come from?

When you and I were born we had few demands. Breath, touch, sleep and some milk were the main ones. We were content with our lot. Since that time we have learnt to deprive ourselves of these basic needs by replacing them with hundreds and hundreds of demands and expectations to make us 'happy'. Since birth our culture and education encourages us to become competitors in the human race. The prize is happiness, but for some reason no one can claim it! Why? It's simple, the race never ends, for if it did you would be happy — content!

Are you a free man or woman, or are you enslaved by the trappings of a culture based on ignorance?

Our ignorance and expectations have confused us and left us chasing a distant mirage called happiness. This chase for happiness ends in emptiness, which in turn increases our demands and expectations. The chase keeps us from being here and now and from fulfilling our real needs, such as good food, warmth, rest and sleep, companionship and compassion. Life then becomes empty and the unattended needs of being human become more desperate. We become melancholic and end up dwelling in the dead past or at best we escape through some addiction into an imagined paradise, only to find ourselves repeating the same pattern unto death. The human being is like a blind man in a dark room, who is looking for a black cat that is not even there! This may seem funny, but the untold suffering in our world is due to this blindness. The question is, how can we wake up to the reality of the situation? What can we do to free ourselves of the addictions and attachments that blind us and bind us to the quest for happiness?

What Are Your Real Needs?

The solution is much simpler than those given to us by the pundits of high society. The answers lie in a common-sense question: "what are your real needs?" You see, addictions and attachment to anything or anyone comes from unfulfilled needs and the more desperate the need, the more desperate the attachment. We suffer, not because we are addicted or attached, but because we do not know how to fulfil the real needs in our lives. This subtle and yet important point must be understood if we are to rid ourselves of the bondage of attachment. The failure to grasp this simple equation could start you on a spiritual journey focused merely on letting go of attachment, rather than also fulfilling one's real physical, emotional, mental and spiritual needs.

We feel uncomfortable and so, like any creature, we try doing something to make the bad feeling go away. A dog who sits on a thorn will stand up. A hungry dog sniffs out food. But humans take a less direct route: for the pain of life's thorns, we take a pain killer; for the hungry, a pill to stop the hunger pangs — and we stay blind to the cause and its proper remedy. You feel bad, take a drink, you feel better! But what really lies behind that bad feeling? Why aren't you automatically as comfortable in the world as a frog or a squirrel? Happiness for humans is simple, just as for frogs and squirrels, so why not move directly to it? Because we receive mistaken knowledge about how to find happiness; we are misinformed by conventional wisdom.

The Wrong Map!

The map is wrong and its route will take you nowhere, driven by frustration and unfulfilled desire. The map of Happy Land has misguided routes and false destinations — a mirage. Yet we hold on to that map, in the form of addictions and attachments, with a desperate grip. We call it our grip on reality. We are convinced. We believe it — because we are told it's so. The funny thing is, we don't actually need a map because what we seek is right here under our own skin! No wonder we can't find it in a can of beer or by driving that new car! Stop the futile search on the endless path, stop — and get to know yourself and your true needs.

Know Your Reality

The purpose of becoming aware is to become conscious of what we need and how to respond to it. Thus consciousness is born out of the limits of our experience and awareness. If you can imagine awareness as a pool, then the reflection you see is the reality of your world. This capacity — to see the world as it is — is our consciousness. All our decisions are made from what we see in the reflection — from the pool of experience and awareness gathered since conception. Because our lives are unique, each one of us sees the world differently. Hence, the image we have of ourselves and the world at large is very different from that of our brother's, sister's, father's, mother's or friend's. This thought, that each one of us sees the world from a different perspective, can be daunting. For what we have understood as 'reality' is only our reality and not other people's.

The Global Game Show

Unlike the human race this journey of life has no prize for the winner. Indeed, there are no winners or losers in this game called life; for life is a game you play, and there is no particular way of playing. The more you play, the more you live, learn and have fun. When we see life as just a global game show, we stop taking ourselves too seriously and lighten up. We begin to take life as it comes and not try to control it. As we get into the game, we become energised and alive. Life simply becomes enjoyable and every day is a new day, full of hope and limitless possibilities. Of course, there are ups and downs, but as on a roller-coaster, you can't have the ups without the downs! It all depends on how you see life.

Every Player Counts

In this chapter, the means and methods we can use to become more aware of our role in the global game show will be explored and in so doing we shall come to realise the importance of every player in the game. Every player counts, for without each one, the game is not complete. Thus, as we become competent players, we can help others improve their game, for the better they play, the better your life becomes! What the world needs now are ordinary people who help each other become aware of the folly of the human race in its quest for happiness. We need to rely on our common sense for within each one of us is all the wisdom of the past, present and future. All we need, is to become aware of it. We need to learn how to access the wisdom that is already in each of us.

The Nature of Knowing

In our society we are born and bred to behave according to the norms and morals laid down by tradition. Almost everything we know and do is guided by traditional values. These norms and values have been passed on from one generation to the next via education and religion in order to maintain stability and continuity within our society. So powerful and persuasive is the nature of tradition that very little has changed at the core of our culture for over a thousand years. So deep are the ways of behaviour and societal expectations ingrained in our psyche that we obey without reason or question. All societies are a reflection of their traditional values, yet no one knows exactly what values, for they vary from one culture to another. What we do know is that traditions are man-made and therefore not to be taken as gospels of truth, beauty, goodness and equality. For if they were, our society would not be rife with crime and corruption, bigotry, poverty, exploitation and homelessness.

Not Knowing

We all know about the immense suffering in our society and complain bitterly, but what part did we play in it, albeit without knowing? We don't know exactly what is causing the suffering or how to change it. For if we did know who or what was responsible and how we came to be in such a mess, we would know how to change it.

> *To know, but not yet to do,*
> *Is not yet to know.*

Chance or Choice?

Why do some people have more opportunities, better education and career, a bright future and better quality of lifestyle? Why is life easier for some and not for others, who despite all their efforts to lift themselves only seem to struggle in vain to a dead end? Is life a chance or a choice? Is your life predestined by class, caste and cultural expectations or is it a 'free for all'?

Why do I ask? *Because life is how you make it.*

Trying Too Hard

When our lives become hard we are conditioned to try harder, but trying harder does not always help. Is it possible, that when life becomes too difficult, it is because we are trying too hard?

Access to Know-how

The question is, how can we get to know new ways of thinking and living when almost everyone we know is stuck in their old ways? How can we know what we don't know? Where do we begin and whom can we ask?

The Way Out!

We begin by learning from a simple occurrence. Imagine some flies have become trapped in an empty bottle. The bottle is in a dark room and there is a candle burning towards the bottom end of the bottle. The flies will keep trying to escape by flying towards the light. They will keep doing this until they eventually die, yet freedom and life are only seconds away!

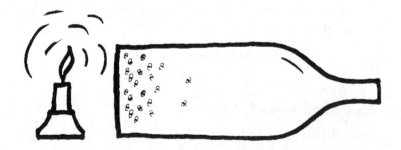

Moving the candle to the other end may initially result in chaos, but the chances are most if not all flies will find their way out. How can you use this analogy in your daily life?

Try this:

First, choose any situation or problem in your life that you have at this moment. Second, ask yourself how you got there. Third, retrace the process instead of trying to break through — for example, if you can't sleep at night, the trick is to stop trying! Whenever we find ourselves suffering, it is often because we are trying too hard. Confucius said, *"The way out is through the door. Why is it that no one uses it?"*

By applying this simple understanding to any problem, we can achieve eternal freedom. The truth is that we are conditioned by society to think and behave in linear ways, and this is why "life's a bitch and then you die", because we don't know any other way. The flies in the bottle analogy can be applied to all realms of human concern where we need to relieve suffering and find solutions to otherwise impossible problems. The trick is to look out of the other end of the bottle — to perceive reality from another direction. In doing this, we allow spontaneity and magic into our lives, and we stop banging our heads against the walls of our own preconditioning.

The Way of Knowing.

Although there are an infinite number of ways that can lead to higher consciousness, there are in my understanding four fundamental ways of knowing. These are: being told, reasoning, imagining and direct knowing. Now, some of you may say that these are obvious and are known throughout the world. But again I can only assume that if they were, the world would be a very different place.

Being told

Being told how to live and what to seek is the most traditional way of knowing. Almost everything we do was shown to us by our parents, teachers, peers and society. All of us learned how to cook, clean, eat, read, write and speak by being shown through the five senses of seeing, hearing, touching, smelling and tasting. Being shown is the most obvious form of learning things, because we can actually see and touch the external world. Its disadvantage, however, lies in the possibility of lives becoming regimented and run by the short-sightedness of those giving the instructions.

The Software of the Mind

The new-born mind is like a warehouse full of empty filing cabinets which the senses will fill with information, but the filing clerk is the perception. Or to be more modern, the infant mind is like a new computer and perception is the software it needs to handle information from the world. We are taught by our family and culture what things mean, or as Hofsteder put it, *"culture is the software of the mind"*.

A human being is a very open and vulnerable creature, especially in its infancy and can be influenced in very deep and profound ways. Children believe that what their parents tell them is the truth; the best way of doing things. Our minds are like huge

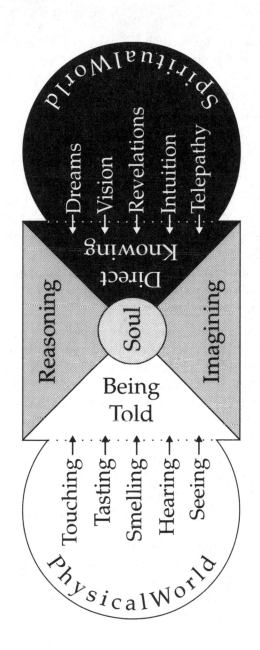

Fundamental sources of knowldege

flexible nets, meant to catch what we need, but they can become clogged up and rigid from the debris of society. Having been told what to do and how to do it, we must apply reasoning to the aim, method and motivation of carrying out the given instruction; be they from our parents, teachers, trainers, commanders, priests or politicians.

This process of reasoning is part of growing up and it enables each one of us to become self-motivated and self-responsible human beings.

Reasoning

Reasoning is making links by asking questions. The links are logical, factual, "if . . . . then". "If I touch the cobra then it will bite me". These "if . . . . then" links form chains of linear thought which can be strong or can bind us to a small, mechanical reality. Science fiction robots use reasoning, but they are not alive and can have no joy in their knowledge.

Reasoning is a simple process of working things out based on what we have experienced and remembered. It involves asking questions and finding answers to solve problems in order to live more comfortably. Our whole society is based on the knowledge we have gained; we are guided by reasoning, which has helped us evolve and progress from being instinctual creatures to human beings.

There are, however, limitations to the scope of reasoning, for it is confined within the space of the existing knowledge and information available. Reasoning alone cannot show us how to get out of trouble or invent and create new things, because to do that we need to project our minds above and beyond our current reality. Any good artist, scientist or social pioneer will tell you that the trick to solving impossible problems is to ask 'unreasonable' questions! All great achievers have the capacity to combine reasoning and imagining, which I call 'imagineering', to work their way forward into the unknown.

Imagining

When we imagine, we create an image of something in our minds — the world has image as its root, but we can also imagine smells, sounds, tastes and touches as well as pictures. Imagine the sound of a bell — a doorbell, or Big Ben. You make it happen inside your mind: it is a conscious act. Where does an image come from? Sometimes it's a memory of something we have experienced: the mind records every sensory impression: you are one huge video recorder! You have tapes you don't even know about, but sound bites and clips will appear at the bidding of your imagination. Sometimes imagination creates something new. When this happens, it's like throwing a handful of memories in the air, and seeing what new, unique pattern they make on landing, like a kaleidoscope. Rarely, what we call 'imagining' isn't a conscious act, but the result of something unconscious, unbidden by our waking selves, bringing to mind images outside our experience: this is direct knowing.

Direct knowing

Direct knowing is perhaps the most difficult to explain because it goes beyond imagining and therefore cannot be explained via language, experience, memory or reasoning. Ironically, what we can say about direct knowing is based on common sense; a sense of knowing which some call a 'gut feeling' ("I just know", or "wow"). The only problem with common sense these days, is that it is no longer common! In our relentless drive to amass money and material wealth, we have focused on the physical world of forms at the cost of ignoring the spiritual, invisible world. We've become experts at measuring quantity, and quantity-based knowledge is respectable, unlike the qualitative, unproved hunch.

Direct knowing is not as ridiculous as it sounds. We often have visions, dreams, premonitions and the same ideas at the same time. When I was a boy, I often heard my mother's voice calling me home from miles away. This kind of direct knowing is called telepathy.

One of the most successful experiments in telepathy was conducted in 1937 by Hubert Wilkins, an Arctic explorer and Harold Sherman, a journalist in New York. Both men were believers in telepathy and agreed to try a long distance test. Three nights a week at 11.30 New York time Wilkins would go over the events of the day in his mind. Three thousand miles away Sherman would try to pick up his thoughts. Whilst radio communication only managed to contact Wilkins in the Arctic thirteen times in five months, Sherman picked up messages weekly and logged even minor occurrences.

The ancient texts are riddled with cases of direct knowing. It appears that humans were more open to direct knowing until a few thousand years ago. In recent years there has been an emergence of the phenomenon referred to as ESP (Extra Sensory Perception). All ESP means is the perception beyond the five senses. Some call it the sixth sense, which I believe is the result of being in tune with our intuitive nature. The way to regain the skill of direct knowing is to believe it is possible. Faith, intuition and making the choice to receive messages is the secret. I discovered the H.E.L.P. pathways via the channel of direct knowing.

The Soul

The whole purpose of knowing is to connect and gain access to one's soul, for without it we are soulless and powerless to do anything. The seat of the soul is where the physical and spiritual worlds meet. All we need do is to remain open to both worlds, and in doing so we come to discover the soul — which is the ultimate purpose of the journey. Although each one's colour, culture and character may be different, what makes us all the same is our soul — hence the saying, *"All people are born equal"*. All the suffering in our world is caused by the denial of one's own soul.

Through the Way of Knowing, we recognise and realise the nature of the soul — the ultimate goal is knowing that we are all one and what I do to you I do to myself. *"Do unto others as you would have done unto yourself."* In knowing that what goes around comes around, we can understand the consequences of our thoughts and actions. The one who really knows the truth lives in accordance with the law: *"All Is One"*.

The N.E.W.S.

Every day we learn something new. Every idea, thought, feeling and action we have, was once new to us. The human mind has a limitless capacity to learn new things. For example, from birth to the age of sixteen we learned how to eat, smile, walk, talk, play games, dance, name colours, smells, people and places, ride a bicycle, make friends, and studied language, math, biology, chemistry . . . Yet, despite our miraculous ability to learn so many things, where has it got us?

When I was a boy, I was fascinated by new ideas, experiences, people and places. Everything I learned seemed wonderful — even magical. For example, someone once told me that there were many other countries in the world. To me this was great *news*! When I was fourteen years of age, I left home to discover these countries . It was wonderful: sights, sounds, places, and people. It was all new, and at the same time I was becoming aware of what was happening in the world. The big picture was revealing itself to me. The one common theme of conversation in all these countries was *the news*. Almost everyone I met talked about issues related to *the news*, so I bought myself a small radio and listened carefully to the news everyday. After a while I too began to discuss issues that were broadcast on the latest news: earthquakes, murder, civil war, corruption, who won the world cup, another Nazi war criminal hunted down.

As I grew into my adulthood, I realised that such discussions had nothing to do with my immediate reality and were in fact making my life miserable. Whenever I saw the news, read the newspaper, watched just about any film, it was being ingrained into my psyche time and time again, just what a terrible world we lived in. Not *knowing* any difference as a teenager, I had believed what I was told and began to view the world according to *the news*. For a period of about ten years I viewed the world as a wicked place. I became ruthless, believing that the only way to survive in this 'cruel world' was to take care of number one — me. I was acting out *the news* from around the world in my personal life! Every story of survival, triumph and defeat was absorbed and in some way acted out. I became very 'strong' and could handle the most adverse conditions while remaining unaffected, even war. In other words, if I could take care of myself in war, I could take care of myself anywhere. Then whilst I was on the front line, I asked myself one simple question. If I was so capable of taking care of number one, could I perhaps help a child, a woman or even humanity?

Later I realised how my view of the world had affected my lifestyle, career, friends and family. I had become hard, rough and tough because I thought it necessary. Don't all young people have to prepare themselves to 'take on' the world? Teenagers are very impressionable.

The TV tells them what the world is doing. I see people bombarded by horrific images every hour, often the same story again and again, until we have learned it like a lesson. This would not be so bad if the stories were good or at least a balance of good and bad. Children see pictures on the news which they would not be allowed to see in a cinema. Whole families eat their dinner between six and eight o'clock whilst watching the most extreme forms of horror our world has to offer. Is it any wonder why our youth are behaving in such unethical and immoral ways?

The news brings us new information. Information is the food of the human psyche. The information which enters our psyche (positive or negative) determines how we use our knowledge. For example, if the news headline reads that the world's banks are controlled by a secret syndicate, then we view the world as corrupt from top to bottom. Corruption then becomes an accepted part of our culture. Beware of the information which enters into your psyche, for the effect is permanent.

I have become weary of *the news*. We are continually being shown just how terrible human beings are to each other and other living creatures. How thoughtless and uncaring we are towards our environment and how violent and wicked the human race really is. This really leads us to fear each other and to feel threatened by those around us and to feel hopeless and helpless. There is a direct connection between what we see and what we do. Quietly observe the reactions of your friends and family when they watch the news.

I don't believe the human race is wicked and uncaring, thoughtless and violent. If you do, then you will have to behave defensively or aggressively every time you are reminded by the wickedness of others. You will in fact become wicked yourself. I am not saying that there is no wickedness in our world. Yes, we have wars, rape, violence, destruction and disease, but if we focus on them all the time, then that is what we shall pro-create. We need a balanced view of the world and that may mean either looking for good news or not watching the news for a while. You see, all information enters into the subconscious which does not know the difference between time and place. The subconscious mind thinks the news is your — its — reality and sends signals to the mind and body. That is why we get affected by horror stories in our living room and even have nightmares.

Now the good news is that humanity is getting more caring and compassionate. It's just that our new consciousness is revealing our horrific past. What is very different now is that people are truly opposed to the horror and in even greater numbers are standing up and saying "no more". More people are working to bring about change. For example, child abuse has always happened but it has only been comparatively recently that we have had organisations like NSPCC. Torture has always happened but we now have Amnesty International. War too, has always been around and even thought of as 'noble'. How many people share that view today? We have more and more people than ever before working in professions that care and help others: nurses, doctors, social workers, vets, firemen, charity volunteers and church workers, etc. Surely with thousands if not millions of people involved in helping each other there must be an abundance of goodness in our world.

Attachment and Awareness

It is generally believed that addictions and attachment are the root cause of all our suffering. For thousands of years, many religions and belief systems have advocated renunciation as a means of freeing oneself from the bondage of eternal suffering. For many centuries monks have retreated to monasteries, ascetics have lived in isolation, and countless ordinary people have tried to rid themselves of their addictions and attachments via the practice of their scriptures.

Despite all this effort, our world is suffering more than ever before. Is renunciation the real solution to freedom from bondage? If not, how can we let go of the possessions and patterns of behaviour that lead to so much sorrow in our lives? The only way to change this dilemma is to become aware of our attachments and to free ourselves from them. How do we go about it?

Considering that most of us are enslaved by our addictions and attachments, we're striving in vain to fulfil some basic need via food, alcohol, sex, material objects, meditation, work, money, power . . . Is it possible that all these things are like bandages that people have used to help heal and mend their broken lives? The real cause of our suffering is due not to addictions and attachment (the symptoms), but because we do not know how we can fulfil our real needs. People have their basic needs and if these needs are not met, a vacuum is left in the body. This is why people are going berserk: nature abhors a vacuum. Ridding ourselves of sensuality and sexuality, material objects and money, will not automatically satisfy our deepest needs or mend our broken lives. The question is, how did we get ourselves in such a mess in the first place?

Just as we use tools to fix things that are not working, in the same way we use chocolate, cocaine, food, fancy cars, clothes, etc., as a fix to make us feel better. Then over a period of time, we become dependent on these. This dependency is referred to as addiction and attachment, because so vital is 'the fix' that we cannot live without it. We can get hooked on anything from masturbation to mountaineering to meditation! The mere thought or threat of losing the fix triggers fear and pain at the most primal levels. So we spend the rest of our lives controlling the patterns and people who supply the fix.

The irony is, that which we control eventually controls us. This is why we end up being victims — prisoners of our addictions and attachments. The solution lies in a common sense question: *"what are my real needs?"* Addictions and attachments come from unfulfilled needs and the more desperate the need, the more desperate the attachment. I once met a big shot guru who told me he had become addicted to the buzz of thousands of followers and needed to keep them by control. I suggested that freedom lay not in renunciation of his position, but in focusing on and fulfilling his basic human needs; such as good food and water, rest and sleep, warmth and shelter, even sensuality and making love which he had denied himself. In nurturing himself, all he was addicted and attached to would drop away like dead leaves in autumn, with no need of renunciation.

Renunciation is a contradiction. It is useless to just say "let go" as it is often suggested. This is like telling someone on a roller-coaster to let go. It is meaningless and may even make matters worse!

Try the following :

1) Be honest. Admit that you are addicted or attached.

    If you cannot live without something or someone you're 'hooked'.

2) Write down why? What is the cause? What is the need?

3) Respond to the need with the real thing.

    In the case of the guru, he needed hugs and kisses from a family, so he collected followers.

4) Be patient.

   As you give yourself plenty of time, the fear of failure will disappear.

Freedom from all suffering lies not in renunciation, but in becoming aware. This subtle and yet important point must be understood if we are to rid ourselves from the bondage that leads to suffering.

Every addiction or attachment is like a stone in one's shoe. Slow down, stop and remove the stone. Behold! Life becomes paradise.

The Role of Knowledge

The Role of Knowledge is to enable humanity to develop and evolve on ever expanding levels. The universe is infinite and so is the human mind and its consciousness. Our consciousness is born within the limits of our awareness. To increase our awareness, we must gain new knowledge. New knowledge gives us new information and insights to unknown possibilities of existence. Hence, the very nature of knowledge is to go where no one has gone before and beyond that!

However, going beyond limits often provokes fear and resistance from the status quo which is why we have taboos in our cultures.

In almost all races and religions there are taboos on certain forms of knowledge. The word 'taboo' means prohibited; it means not being allowed to go beyond or to gain access to certain knowledge.

There are four areas which are commonly taboo in most cultures.

Knowledge via Nature Worship

Over billions of years our bodies and minds have evolved to what we are now. We are a result of the evolutionary process guided by nature. All primitive cultures worshipped nature and gained their power and wisdom from it. The word worship means to serve and respect. Today, nature worship is taboo. Instead we dominate and rape the natural world. Is it possible that our attitude towards nature and the way we treat it is actually causing the suicide of humanity, and the genocide of other species?

To begin with, we must relearn to witness nature and envision the human place within it. To view the wilderness as alive and everything in nature as living, encompassing the wind, water, rocks, mountains and so on as parts of the whole living being that is the earth. The earth gave birth to us and it is our privilege to be custodians of this unique planet. In order for us to be custodians of the earth we must become keepers of the knowledge contained in the wilderness.

Knowledge Via Sex

Sex is probably the most important driving force in all species, including human beings. From the dawn of creation sex has played a critical role in the evolutionary journey of humankind. Without it you and I would not be here. Our bodies and minds contain billions of particles and limitless information all of which was passed on via sex. Sex, it can be said, is the most primal form of communication.

Yet, sex is the least talked about subject in most circles, especially within our families, schools and churches. Why? Where else are we to discuss such a powerful and beautiful form of communication? Animals and primitive societies have sex freely and guiltlessly, whilst we in the modern world are inhibited and unfulfilled sexually. The results are profoundly destructive not only to ourselves but also to the earth.

We must reconnect with our sexuality and let go of the fear and shame that contaminates the innocent act of sex. Unlike animals, we have the capacity to develop our sexuality in infinite creative ways via discussion, fantasy, art, erotica, etc. Sex is a silent language that relays subtle and powerful forces. It can be said that to have sex with one woman or man is to have sex with all women and men everywhere. The secret of mastering the power of sex is to use it as a channel of service.

Knowledge Via Mysticism

Each one of us has mystical experiences: deja-vu, precognitive dreams, synchronicity and deep intuition. The secret to knowledge through mysticism is not to try and explain life rationally and analytically — this is a contradiction in terms! The secret is to simply recognise that the many unexplainable moments that one has in life are normal and healthy. Life does not have to make sense all the time!

For example, when we have a dream or a nightmare, it is a mystical experience. Although we can try to explain the dream rationally, we are left with a very limited expression of the total experience. When we analyse a mystical experience, we have to use language which is not only in its infancy when compared to the complex human brain, but also a tool of the physical world — not the metaphysical. Metaphysical means beyond the physical. To unlock the doors to the metaphysical, the supernatural realm, we can use intuition. Intuition gives us access to mystical knowledge which is beyond our physical reality. Like any other form of knowledge, mystical knowledge can be used or abused.

The history of humanity has been a battle between the forces of 'good and evil'. This battle has its roots in the mystical psyche of the individual and collective consciousness. All the conflict in one's world can be transformed into everlasting peace by becoming aware of the mystical realm. The aborigines call it 'dream time' – a mystical tradition which can be traced back over forty thousand years. Like the aborigines we need to develop our understanding of the mystical realm and introduce the knowledge to our young people.

Knowledge Via Truth

Truth is the supreme secret in our society. The state and the church, the police and secret services keep the truth from us, supposedly for our own good. The irony is, the truth sets us free. Is it possible that people are not free, because those in power do not want us to be free? The question is, how do we gain access to the truth? In the East they say *"There is your truth, my truth and the truth"*. So, even if the people in power tell us the truth, it is only their version of it.

What we want is not the truth proclaimed by priests, politicians and philosophers, but the truth. What is that truth? Who decides what the absolute truth is? Over thousands of years we have been brainwashed in believing in the truths handed down by the scriptures and enforced by people in power. Why should you and I abide by the truth proclaimed centuries ago? Our capacity to live the truth is stunted by our inability to question and discover it ourselves.

For example, many people believe in the existence of God not because they have experienced it for themselves but because they have been told that it is the truth. What if there is no God as portrayed by the church? What would happen to the religious empires that exist today, if this were so? Can the truth be explained in the scriptures or in a sermon? When Jesus was asked, *"What is the truth?"*, he remained silent.

No one can or should tell another what the truth is. Humanity is suffering because we are unknowingly trying to live out the truth handed to us by others. The 'truth' has become a tool for keeping the status quo; not for setting people free. The secret of gaining access to the truth is not to search for it. Follow no one and you will find whatever truth there is to find.

The Power of Patience

When I was a boy, my mother once said to me *"drop by drop lakes are created"*, which is a very old proverb of Sanskrit origin. Then, in my teenage years when I was travelling through Rome, I saw on the Vatican wall, an old emblem saying *"Festina Lente"* which in Latin means *"Go fast, slowly"*. Intuitively I knew what these words meant, for I felt their power in my body. Yet, as I grew up into manhood, I slowly and gradually forgot my mother's words and the power they brought to me.

Over the next decade I embarked on big projects that required immense effort, which drained me to the point of exhaustion. I had become powerless and the cause was impatience. I had, in fact, become a puppet of the fast moving, instant world we live in — a clatter of noises and senseless actions. Not only had I become powerless due to my impatience, it was humiliating to watch myself try to cover up my stupidity by behaving patiently.

The truth was my impatience had eaten away at the core of my being and all the knowledge and wisdom I had in my head was useless. The way forward was simple. I had to be more patient. To do that meant giving up all that which was making me impatient. It was a Catch 22 situation: I was powerless within, for the lack of patience, and I would be powerless without for letting go of these projects. Either way I would end up powerless. Having no choice, I surrendered!

The Power of Patience

Surrendering all forms of power is the most powerful thing we can do. It is the practice of patience in its purest form that gives us access to the absolute power of wisdom. Without patience there can be no wisdom and hence no power. This is why patience is one of the most important elements in our lives. Patience gives us the wisdom to choose wisely and the power to change the face of events. Hence the proverb, *"Patience is a virtue"*!

The more patient we become, the less we force ourselves and others to achieve. We simply live and let live and everything falls into place as though by magic.

Sitting quietly doing nothing;

Spring comes and the grass grows by itself.

The practice of patience gives us magical powers, for it makes everything possible. No matter what it is we want to do, the moment we apply patience, it is guaranteed to happen sooner rather than later. Most people fail to achieve what they set out to do because they give up or simply burn out by going too fast. The following example provides valuable insights into the practice and power of patience.

The Chinese bamboo is planted and must be watered every day. A week, two weeks, a month, two months and three months go by and nothing happens. Four months, five months and six months and still nothing happens. Then, after six months, during a period of six weeks, it grows from seed to twenty-eight feet!

Shakespeare said, *"To climb steep hills requires slow pace at first"*. The central message of all these examples is that patience is a virtue that makes everything possible, be it learning to play a sport or learning to play a musical instrument, bringing up children, finding a cure for a disease, or bringing peace and prosperity to the world. Patience makes the impossible . . . possible, and doing the impossible is the wisdom to make miracles. All miracles have one thing in common — they are not forced.

The Significance of Knowing

The sole purpose of the knowledge contained in this book is meant to enable ordinary people to improve their whole lives. I hope that in this chapter you have gained new insights, ideas and information to make practical changes in the way you live. After all, the way we live is a reflection of the knowledge we have and the way we use it. When knowledge is used consciously — purposefully — it becomes knowing. A lot of people tend to amass knowledge as with wealth, but live out lost, loveless lives. They lack the knowing of what knowledge is for. So what is knowledge for?

The role of knowledge is to know how to live.

The most important thing in life is living itself. Most people tend to forget that and focus their minds (knowledge) on other things like cars, careers, sport, business, politics, profit, power...

Each day we allow our minds to be bombarded by a whole barrage of things from all directions. During this onslaught it's all too easy for us to end up lost and confused, running around like blue-arsed flies. The human race is moving too fast, the individual cannot focus on the real priorities. The following method shows how you can apply knowledge to get from here to there— wherever there is for you.

Method:

I have found that there are two basic responses to life. Escape or explore. The latter is a source of knowledge. There are four steps we can use to transform knowledge into knowing.

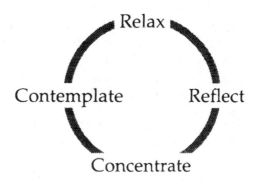

1) Relax

Free the body and mind from tension. This can be done in many ways such as walking, breathing, stretching, sitting quietly, bathing, sleeping, making love, swimming, being massaged . . . When we are rested we feel peaceful and content.

2) Reflect

Look at life as a spectator watching a game. Just like a calm lake, reflecting the shortest blade of grass to the whole sky. Let your mind become like a mirror to see clearly.

3) Concentrate

Choose an object, experience or aim. This will reduce the number of thoughts, superficial speculations, useless activities and distractions. What you focus on will happen to you. Concentrate on what you really need and want.

4) Contemplate

Ponder on what matters quietly and honestly. Ask yourself how you can use the knowledge you have gained to help yourself and others. For example, choose a part of your life which you want to improve. Then apply the insights you have gained from the analogy of the flies in the bottle. From insight, come solutions and then action. This is knowledge transfered into knowing.

The way of knowing is a way to insert life into our lives. It presents the key skills to harness the beauty and joy of living with a vision, purpose and a sense of our own priorities. In short, to see the wood from the trees. We can then concentrate on what we love. Knowing brings about a clarity of mind and a sense of direction and well-being, without which we can become lost. This sense enhances our capacity to focus on life itself and to experience it fully and enjoyably. For what a person does is not as important as the way they do it.

It's not what you do;
It's the way that you do it!

Making Changes

For Example

INSIGHT: I am suffering because I have neglected the foundations of my life.

SOLUTION: From now onwards I will focus only on my health, home, family and creativity.

ACTION: This Saturday I will cook myself a healthy meal and eat it peacefully.

INSIGHT:

SOLUTION:

ACTION:

INSIGHT:

SOLUTION:

ACTION:

INSIGHT:

SOLUTION:

ACTION:

The Way of Relating

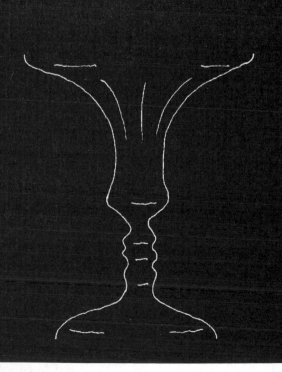

How well does each statement describe your pattern of thought and action?

- *I have a variety of satisfying relationships.*
- *I freely give and receive love and support.*
- *I enjoy touching and sharing physical and spiritual contact with others.*
- *I am comfortable with the feminine and masculine parts of myself.*
- *I have meaningful relationships with people of all ages including children and elders.*
- *I am in harmony and share affection with the people I work with.*
- *I feel a deep respect for my friends and family.*
- *I am free from fear and guilt and am completely honest with myself and others.*
- *I am free from revengeful thoughts and actions.*
- *I have realised that lying equals dying.*
- *I know how to transform conflict creatively.*
- *I treat everyone the same, and respect everyone I meet — rich and poor, wise and foolish, black or white, male or female, etc.*
- *I know how to handle resistance from people wisely.*
- *I can remain honest and centred in the midst of deception and treachery.*
- *I am part of a group or community where I have gained respect for fulfilling my responsibilities over a long period of time.*
- *I take enough time to be alone and nurture myself.*
- *I know how to listen.*
- *I have a positive image of myself and express myself freely.*
- *I am accepting of non-orthodox forms of relationships: homosexuality, bisexuality, celibacy, extended families, etc.*
- *I am open to new ways of relating to people, animals and nature.*

Introduction

We humans are social creatures. We invest so much of our time and energy in relationships at home, at work, with friends in the clubs and pubs, yet, the lack of fulfilling relationships, coupled with widespread loneliness, is one of the main causes of social strife in our time. Ironically, it is loneliness — a deep need for belonging — which drives even the most capable of individuals to substance abuse or to fall for the strangest partners in a desperate attempt to fill the gaping hole in their heart. Others feel disconnected from the vast society they live in and therefore remain alone, hoping in their quiet moments to meet like-minded people through a chance meeting on a bus, train or plane.

As our cities have grown in scale, the traditional community ties have weakened and so have the individual's means of supportive relationships. Most people, even the rich and famous, live lonely lives, crying out to escape the reality of their emptiness caused by the fear of a predatory world. Those who are not able to cope commit acts of self-abuse. Is it any wonder that every thirty-five seconds another person tries to commit suicide? The way out of this dilemma is to get out and meet people. The most important thing in any society is that people stay connected, not only with each other but with creation as a whole. Staying connected entails opening one's heart and home to those with whom you want to have an intimate relationship.

There is no such thing as a loner, for everyone would like to have at least one intimate, committed and fulfilling relationship. However, most intimate relationships are short-lived and fail. Why? The primary cause for this failure is a widespread lack of relationship know-how. As infants we were taught how to use a potty. At school we were taught maths, geography, science, and history. As adults we learn how to drive a car, pay taxes, build skyscrapers and empires, play golf and produce high-tech societies, and yet we are crippled or handicapped when it comes to the challenge of dealing with adult relationships. Most of us learn about relationships simply by having them and most of us learn the hard way — by repeated trial and error. When, in time, we come to what is usually the central, most important partnership of adult life — an enduring and fulfilling relationship — we are all too often ill-prepared. Everywhere we look we see troubled and torn relationships. Today forty per cent of marriages end up in divorce. Broken families are only a part of the overall picture in the current battleground of human relationships. Relationships in all sectors of our community are falling apart. People are at each other's throats and because of the highly competitive culture we live in, we have little or no time for each other. The need to live up to the next fad or fashion is deemed more important than making new friends. We expect people to live up to fantasy images of perfection. We expect that we ourselves must be perfect in order to be loveable or attractive and seek the equivalent perfection in partners and friends.

The pressure is tremendous — look at magazines, exhorting you daily to be this or to look like that, encouraging you to lose your individuality and become a facsimile of some mass produced ideal. If you don't love yourself as you really are right now, how can you relate intimately to another person? How do you know if the person you are relating to is really her/himself, or if they are striving to put on some acceptable mask, supposedly to make you love them? If these fundamental aspects are distorted, then so will be the relationship. Although the pressure to relate falsely is tremendous, we have become so used to it that it has become no more apparent than gravity! This pressure to live up to societal expectations is a major cause of the breakdown of family and society.

People seem to think that relationships grow by themselves and that they need not be cultivated. Personal relationships are so much a part of human existence that we have a natural tendency to take them for granted. Yet when we look at a relationship, like any other growing thing, we see that the better it is cared for, the better it grows. How many people ever stop to think, really think, about their relationships, what they amount to, how they are developed and how they could improve? We adopt a consumer attitude to our relationships: if it's not right, get a new one! Most, as a result, deny themselves reachable joys: the deep satisfaction that whole-hearted commitment brings, and the high-points of happiness and self-fulfilment that come with true intimate relationships.

Sound information about making the most of relationships is hard to acquire casually. Often adults with relationship problems do not talk about them with others who could learn from their experience, and those adults in happy relationships, thoughtful though they may be, seldom formulate principles they could pass on to others in conversation. The most common problem people seek counselling for is relationships. However, relationships in general, and couple relationships in particular (with the Royal Family in the forefront), have become a new focus of society at large.

The fact is, whatever it is that you want to create or are looking for, the chances are you will need to handle relationships to get it. This chapter is especially designed to make it easy and pleasurable to do so. It will help you to find out how to resolve relationship problems as well as to create new and fulfilling relationships. Although the main focus is on practical ways of enriching personal relationships, the same principles and methods can be applied in most professional settings. Relationships with animals and other life-forms are vital too.

As you apply the knowledge within to your relationships, at first you will experience peace and then more prosperity. Peace, because knowingly or unknowingly you will be taking the path of least resistance. As you learn how to handle the challenges of adult relationships, there will be less resistance in your life. The way of least resistance will enable you to accomplish your goals more easily and gracefully. Wherever you wander, peace and prosperity will surround you. Because of the way you care for people, miracles will take place, for the secret of achieving the impossible lies in the way we relate to people. When that happens, you have transformed knowledge into action — a labour of love! In doing so you have inherited the most important thing people can give — their labour of love.

The Nature of Relating

As I sat quietly at a small beach named Sandymouth in Cornwall, staring out across the horizon, I felt myself a part of the sky, sun, sea, clouds, wind and the earth underneath my body. I cannot explain in words what I felt, as everything I felt there is to feel in the moment. I have had this feeling many times since my childhood, with such completeness, that nothing mattered and everything mattered; I was alone and yet together with everything.

This experience is the best example I can think of to begin exploring the nature of relating to anyone or anything. For me, relating has been a mystical experience — mystical because I've always been amazed how so many people and diverse events enrich my life as if by magic. Magic or miracle is the nature of relating; the crashing of waves on the beach, birds singing, rainbows, dowsing for water . . . all come from 'miraculous' events. I have felt that all I need for miracles to happen to me, is to be open and willing to relate to nature, animals and people. Hence, when I talk about relating, what I mean is the interplay of life with oneself. It appears that all things, from the atom to the amoeba, are part of one miraculous living organism we call earth. Choose any one event, or item, such as the birth of a baby, a volcano, a flower, a grain of rice or a colour, and behold, we are witnessing a miracle. A flower really is miraculous when you consider the odds against such a tiny seed surviving, and its beauty is transcendent. Relating is our capacity to taste, smell, touch, hear, see, feel and appreciate whatever is happening in and around us.

In order for us to relate fully, we need to open all our senses, heart and psyche to fully experience the event as it happens. In other words, the more we are open, the more we are open to life. The aim of life is to be in it. Problems begin when we close ourselves to the world and become disconnected from the source. The fact is, nothing can live in isolation and the more we try to live in isolation, the more we suffer. Relating is being totally open, vulnerable. It is dangerous because it means letting go of the formulas and footholds we have used to resist relating to the world.

We are told to take control or take charge of our lives, consequently we keep ourselves under control at all times and maintain a steady voice. Often, what our culture refers to as 'graceful' or 'spiritual' behaviour is nothing other than a mastery of self-denial, indifference or a form of deadness. Public figures often do not let their feelings out, they deny themselves the use of all their natural, direct outlets, such as crying, laughter, anger and passion. They may be afraid to show their vulnerability to their followers and opponents or to open any of the outlets, for fear that all their stored-up feelings will come bursting out uncontrollably.

When our channels of relating are closed, we become full, and when we remain dangerously full for a long time, the body instinctively finds an indirect outlet for the feelings. A well-behaved youth may suddenly leave home or become severely depressed. A smooth-talking businessman may develop an ulcer, or drink heavily to relieve his tension. A well balanced therapist, healer or spiritual teacher may find refuge in unseen fixes such as excessive meditation, masturbation, or self-importance. One way or another, the day comes when the need to remain closed becomes so painful that we risk opening. Remember the lotus flower which grows in murky waters, yet so open and pure.

More and more people are now coming out of the shells lived in before them by their forebears. They look like the dead rising from their graves. The open earth, the open sky, welcome them, and so can I with my open heart.

The Whole Heart

Opening oneself is like dying, just as a seed must die to become a plant. This feels dangerous, because we will not remain the same. We cannot control it. Much of who we thought we were will fall away. We can let go bit by bit or jump; open our hearts slowly, or let them burst open like flood gates. It does not really matter because the aim is to live wholeheartedly. This, of course, is easier said than done, for where is there a safe place or person with whom we can be wide open with our heart on view? People who force themselves to be wide open, often hurt themselves and then close down even more.

Living wholeheartedly sounds very nice, but how can we comprehend what it means? How do we do it? In my experience, living wholeheartedly comes from direct experience and as such it cannot be learned from a book, story, or in a seminar. This wisdom of living wholeheartedly can be demonstrated and therefore passed on from one to another. It begins by finding a place and persons who are willing to be completely open, without fear and guilt. Being in a safe place or in the company of someone who is safe will soothe the fear of the unknown. For example, when we are in nature we feel safe and yet nature uses no force or fancy words to find its way into our heart.

We can begin to open our hearts in nature. You could go to a sacred place and listen. A sacred place is one where the earth's voice can be heard more clearly. Once you have heard her, she can reach you anywhere.

Nature is neutral and without judgement of good or bad, beauty or ugliness. It lets us be who we are, which is why we feel safe to let nature into our heart. As a boy, I spent long periods in nature by myself and had a mother who encouraged me to absorb and value the nature of nature. I now realise that the feeling of being at one comes firstly with our heart-to-heart connection with oneself, with other people and with nature — our fundamental teacher.

"Speak to the earth and it shall speak with thee."

These days, most people live in towns or cities and it is difficult for many to see how to relate to nature. Yet even in cities, nature is all around us. From the tiny plants poking through cracks in a wall, to the pigeons on the street. And in our homes, nature provides everything we need, from the kitchen table to our jeans. Nature gives us everything unconditionally: should we not repay such love with love?

The first step is to be aware of the precious gifts of nature; the second step is to be thankful for them and to use them wisely, never wastefully. In wholeheartedly accepting nature as part of us and part of everything, the unity of life becomes apparent, and relating becomes easier.

> *The thoughts of the earth are my thoughts.*
> *The voice of the earth is my voice.*
> *All that belongs to the earth belongs to me.*
> *All that surrounds the earth surrounds me.*
> *It is lovely indeed, it is lovely indeed.*
>
> Navajo song.

The Way of Relating

A relationship is a living thing, and just like every living thing it has a cycle and a process. If we are to have any idea of what is happening in our relationships, we need to know how they work and how to develop them. There are infinite activities or interactions that form relationships, yet there are four stages that seem to appear in all realms of human interplay. Meeting, investigation, integration and intimacy play off each other to create a continuum we call life. The cycle or spiral of relating is an ongoing process and these four stages are active within and without us throughout our lives.

Meeting is the first stage of any relationship, be it with a dog, dolphin or person. The initial contact or initiation with something or someone new is a very mysterious happening, for so many different events, decisions, failures and successes have brought us to the point of meeting. Some people call it chance, or luck, fate or fortune, synchronicity or destiny. Whatever it is, the potential of a new encounter with another has enormous power and the way we use it can lead us to prosperity or poverty. This is why we say *"first impressions are lasting impressions"*, for what happens between us in the initial milli-seconds is connected to our deepest thoughts, feelings and preferences. When we meet someone for the first time, we have ventured into the unknown. Going into the unknown triggers off all kinds of reactions and responses as we try to make head or tail of who or what we are dealing with.

What makes you choose this person rather than that one? Something about the person attracted you. Attraction between people is the first stage of relating, whether it's friendship, business or sex. We speak of chemistry, of some mysterious force like magnetism that draws some people together just as it repels others. On the whole, we have a tendency to label people according to their colour, creed, clothing or career. But is that all that we are? We all believe we want to be attractive, yet what is it that attracts? Is it something in the person you meet or something in yourself?

People give off subtle signals constantly, sending messages with body language or dress, but these have to be received in order for attraction to take place. In other words you have to be looking for something in order to see it! So attraction is as much about your needs and desires as about the other person's qualities. Much of what we think we want from our relationships is social garbage, the psycho-babble of mass media. Taoists say, *"Desire can never be satisfied"* — no matter how much you eat, you'll always feel hungry again later. Your desires are frequently either manufactured by media, culture and convention or they are false trails leading you to frustration: what you want isn't necessarily the same as what you need.

Our ears clamour with wants, but need speaks in a quiet voice. Relationships fail because needs aren't met, because we lack knowledge of our own and other's needs. You may think you want a partner who looks like a model and has a lifestyle of a high-flyer, but you may need gentleness, humour and inspiration. We act like consumers, shopping in the human supermarket for the latest life accessory, dazzled by the hype, the superficial, the novel and the tasty, luxurious tit-bits, and end up with a malnourished heart, starved of the basic nourishment of relationships — love.

Investigation is the second stage, where we begin to explore the nature of our relationships, lying below or beyond the surface of our persona. We start to look a little bit closer, and closer! With the investigation process, there appear to be three main depths that form the 'pool' of the human condition.

The first is superficial, where we find out each other's homes, jobs, tastes in music, etc. . .

The second is usually hidden from most, and only a few select individuals are privileged to enter that depth, and even then they cannot stay there. This is where we keep our hidden agendas, phobias and fantasies.

The third, the deepest part of the person, is usually out of bounds and no one, including oneself, is allowed to enter this space. All kinds of memories in the form of fears, phobias, pain, resentments are at the bottom of the pool. As we get older, the junk at the bottom of the pool increases and we become masters at laying decoys to keep people from investigating this part of the pool. My question is, what have we done which is so bad that we cannot let others know about it? Before all the junk was ditched there, what else existed there and is it buried underneath layer after layer of personal and societal garbage? In all these years of working with people, I have never come across a person whose 'bad actions' even remotely outweighed the 'good ones'! Even the lives of the most tyrannical despots, when investigated on a day-to-day basis, portray kindness, joy, humility and compassion to their loved ones. The trick of preventing 'bad actions' is to let ourselves and others come into our private spaces and look around, for there are gems and pearls to be found under the garbage.

Intimacy is the next stage in the relating process. Let me clarify what I understand from my experience of intimacy. My definition of intimacy is seeing and feeling without thinking, for the moment I think about what I see and what I feel, I stop being intimate. The nature of the mind is to think about things; we are thinking about what we see and feel. Intimacy is about feeling; it's about being. Thought takes us one step away from being; it makes us evaluate and think about it. Consequently, we are always one step away from being intimate. So if I want to be intimate with you and I want to hug you, if I think about hugging you then . . . I think about hugging you! Intimacy is not about thinking of giving you a hug, it's about hugging you — that's what makes the experience intimate. In our relationships we always look for different kinds of intimacy, such as physical, mental and spiritual intimacy. All of us want to connect with our partners, parents and friends on an intimate level; yet thinking prevents us from doing so.

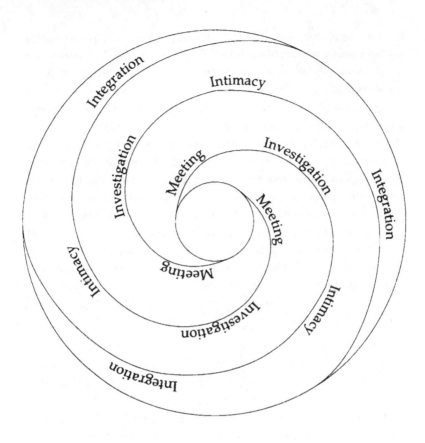

The evolutionary spiral of relationships

When you see a chance to be intimate, take it. If you're thinking, you will keep thinking forever. The aim is just to approach the person and say, *"Do you know what fear is? Well, I am afraid now because I'd like to give you a hug"* and then do it! The most versatile channel of intimacy I know is a hug. You can hug in any and all relationships, from a friend, your father or mother, sister or brother, your teacher or a tree, your president or your guru.

You can do it to them all. The good thing about hugging is that it brings people so close to each other that you can't actually see one another's 'faults'! When we hug someone, for a few seconds we loose ourselves and become one .

Integration is the final stage in the cycle. As we have seen, when two people meet, they investigate and come close to each other, and finally integrate each other's characters. People are like revolving entities in time and space. They are like squares, triangles, hexagons, pentagons and as they come close to each other, the edges touch or hit and produce certain sounds like Ooch, Awh, Pow, Wham, Ooh, Aahh! Every time the shapes meet each other, an edge gets chipped off part of the ego. Sometimes the collisions are too much and we need time and space to recover. As the process continues, the entities become rounder and ultimately both revolve in harmony.

By harmony, I mean the capacity to get on with each other — not behaving like a fart doesn't stink! If our understanding of integrated relationships is that of 'nice nice', i.e. without disagreements, we shall never learn and evolve as human beings, relating in a real sense. There are always going to be disagreements and sometimes major collisions which are part of the integration process. There is often frustration prior to total integration, because we cannot 'break through' or relate fully, due to reasons still unknown. However, sooner or later we start to feel things 'coming together' in our relationships, where two become one and then become two again.

Integration is a critical step of any relationship, for the failure to do so results in destruction. The ego often gets in the way, for becoming one with another represents a threat to one's identity. This is why integration leads to transformation. Evolution has relied heavily on integration as a means to perpetuate life from the dawn of creation. If we look at nature every atom, molecule, element and creature somehow manages to get on with each other.

Integration requires a delicate balance between removing barriers between yourself and others, and maintaining healthy boundaries to your own individual identity. False integration occurs when we fall in love, i.e. when we lose ourselves in the relationship. To hide inside a relationship is self-denial and this stunts the growth of both partners. We are merely projecting our desires on to our partner, ignoring the reality of who or what they are. To perceive falsely another as part of us denies their freedom of will, their freedom to grow. True integration honours and nurtures individuality. It promotes the spiritual growth of the other person; when you do that for someone else, you automatically do it for yourself too. Both parties grow and evolve through interdependency. Anything else leads to unfulfilling relationships and suffering!

The Role of Conflict

Sooner or later, conflict enters into every relationship. It often arises when partners become aware of incompatibility between each other's actions or goals. For relationships to work, we need to have a healthy attitude towards conflict and to make premeditated agreements on how the conflict will be resolved. Conflict can be destructive or constructive. If we use it to explore our values, blind spots and possibilities, we can make compromises and strengthen the commitment to our partner and to our relationship. In this sense, constructive conflict is a natural and vital part of a relationship's growth, whereas destructive conflict can stagnate and destroy relationships. Most relationships break down because people do not know how to use conflict creatively and positively.

The word conflict means a fight, struggle, collision, clashing of principles etc. The secret of resolving all conflict lies in the awareness of what causes it. All conflict is caused by the meeting of opposites or polarities, i.e. positive and negative, good and bad, war and peace. Polarity simply means the other side. We all have polarities within ourselves. For example, male and female, inhale and exhale, asleep and awake. In the same way we have polarities in our metaphysical make up, such as kindness and cruelty, grace and disgrace, greed and generosity, intelligence and stupidity.

We tend not to be aware of both. Some people only see the good sides, others see only bad. This is somewhat like viewing the moon; we can only see the light side and not the dark.

What you see — acknowledge about yourself — is the light side. The conflict occurs when the light and dark sides meet. This can happen in infinite ways. For example, if I believe that I am very smart and never stupid, then when someone points out my stupidity, conflict will arise; the moment I acknowledge my stupidity, conflict will dissolve. Hence, all conflict in relating, be it within our family, with friends, other people or between nations, is a result of not being able to acknowledge and embrace our own polarities. Instead, we tend to point the finger and blame others. It is better to fight "the devil outside than the devil inside." All the conflict in the world including the fight between good and evil is caused by the conflict within us. Whenever you are in conflict, look within and you'll find its source and solution.

The following steps can be used to resolve conflict and use it as an opportunity for growth.

Step 1   Encourage both sides to become aware of their own darker sides and mistakes. You have to know your own dark side! That shadow you run from throughout life: embrace it!

Step 2   How do you hear complaints about yourself? Learn to listen.

Step 3   Ask yourself how you can resolve the conflict without making your partner defensive.

Step 4   Ask how can you work out your differences, even if it means compromise.

Our society is basically afraid of conflict, because it can disturb the norm. We think that if we allow conflict to surface, it will become chaos and ultimately anarchy. In fact, if we actually examine the cause of anarchy, it is not due to an open and mature attitude towards conflict but to a denial or an agreed social suppression of the very existence of conflicting opinions and actions. When we control conflicting opinions or suppress them, it inevitably leads to revolution and anarchy.

We are so afraid of conflict that we try to avoid differences and see uniformity and conformity as peaceful and desirable. Differences are valuable – "Vive la difference!". Harmony can't exist without differences: harmony is a pleasing combination of different musical notes. Harmony in relationships is only possible if there are differences that in combining produce a more pleasant depth than like meeting like. The same repeating note in music is monotonous. Again, as in music, some differences jar unpleasantly; are incompatible. However, unlike pianos, we can change our tunes! We can move position, give some ground, compromise and accommodate the differences between ourselves and another person.

The Power of Words

By the end of today, we will have used thousands of words to think, speak and work out ways of getting things done. Yet, how much do we know about the power of words? Most of us are very careful about what we put into our mouths, but do we watch what comes out of it?

We relate to each other and the outside world via the use of words, be they spoken or written. Every word we use begins its journey as a thought form and ends up as a physical form. For example, everything you see around you was once an idea or thought in someone's head. Think of an idea. Now see how many words are contained within it. Ideas are highly charged particles which contain thousands of words and images. Ideas, images and words form our imagination — the scissors of the mind. With them we can change and create new realities in our daily lives.

Imagine an enormous wardrobe-wordrobe in your mind filled with words you use to cloth yourself. Now look at the way you choose your clothes everyday. Do you wear the shabby ones first and save the better for later? "Eat the speckled apple first", was *thought* to be the highest of *wisdom*. What they did not understand was that this wisdom would never allow them to eat the *good* apples, for they too would be speckled by the time they eat them. If that is the way you use words, then every idea you have will be based on the same wisdom. Is it any wonder why so many people never catch up with their *good*? Words and thoughts must be handled with wisdom and understanding.

Your consciousness may be crammed with destructive thoughts, but by continually using *good* words you will dissolve these negative thought forms into positive ones. The moment you start using *good* words *good* things will happen to you. How does it work? The spoken word is not only a symbol, but also a sound-vibration. For example, when you speak the word 'good', the word good implies many things that make you feel good. The sound of a word can also make you feel good or bad, just as the sound of musical notes can. Just as the musician is the first to hear the sound: the speaker is the first to feel the effect of the word.

If we look at the power of the word in this way, even the thought of telling a single lie makes us shudder. Fear, greed, impatience and mistrust forces people to use words in ways which are destroying them and their society. For example, a lie is like taking a suicide pill. A lie stems from fear and fear destroys the immune system. A lot of the dis-ease, developed within the body of humanity will disappear when dishonesty is replaced by honesty.

The secret of life and death is in the word.

Every word you speak sends vibrations into the world, which come back to you. Look back in your life and you will find that what has happened to you and your family is a result of what you have believed, thought, said and loved. This may sound farfetched, but how else have you arrived in your current condition?

This is how it works. Whatever you believe, think, say and love is done via the use of words — a vibratory force which activates the law of attraction. So, if you believe that you are precious, then you will become precious. If you think that you can create a beautiful home, so you shall. If you say, "I want love", you will be loved. The 'word' is the source of creation, for it says in the bible that "*In the beginning was the word, and the word was made flesh*". That is the power of words.

Forgiveness and Acceptance

From the moment of waking in the morning until going to sleep at night, there are moments in the day in which we consciously or unconsciously recall memories from yesterday, last week, last month, ..., right back to our very first impression of life in the womb. In fact, everything that has happened to us has been stored in our memory. We store up within ourselves the memories which then influence our judgement of people and the conditions we create.

Our memory is like a mirror. What we see in the mirror is who we are. Who we are then determines the way we feel and how we see the world. If you feel hate and resentment, you see enemies in the world. If you feel happy and loving, you see friends. In other words, everything you see and everyone you meet is your mirror. Ironically, what we see inwardly or outwardly is projected on to the world outside in the form of actions and deeds. The world outside then reacts to us in the same way. This is called karma, or come-back.

For example, if you have hated or hate someone now, then hate will beset you. If you have helped or help someone now, then help will come upon you. He who condemns will bring condemnation upon himself. How many of us would like happy and harmonious lives? What can we do to live in a world of peace and ease? There is never going to be a chance for us to know peace or paradise until we have completely forgiven our enemies.

But what exactly is forgiveness? The truth is there is no such thing as forgiveness by others, us or a god. There is only the realisation of what has happened and acceptance of it. This is really the true idea of forgiveness. There is really no sin to forgive, for good and evil are a state of mind, an illusion. There really is no god to forgive us. When the state of consciousness which could be born of hate, resentment, guilt, jealousy, malice , etc., 'dies', there not only is nothing to forgive, and nobody to forgive, there is not even a remembrance or memory of the act: forgive and forget ! When we accept ourselves completely, we embrace everything and everyone. We become one with the world. Until we reach that state of consciousness, we are blocked within and continue to be under the penalty of sin and guilt.

For those who cannot forgive, there is another way. You see, all sins come from want. Even wanting to forgive is a form of wanting. For example, what would happen if the Jews did not even try to forgive the Germans for the holocaust?

What would happen if you simply did not focus a single thought on trying to forgive those who have 'done you wrong'? Is the desire to forgive a result of judgement based on good and evil?

If so, then when there is no judgement, there is no need for forgiveness. For example, when we were children, we had little or no idea of good and evil and so our judgement of others was non-existent. We have since then learned how to judge and forgive. The way to unlearn how to judge and forgive is simply to forget — do not give it a single thought.

You know the saying, "A dog is a man's best friend"?. That is so, because the dog forgets what happened yesterday, last week and so on. How wonderful would it be if we too could forget all trespasses against us. Then, perhaps we could look out on this world, and with our new vision behold a world in which there is not a thing anyone has that we want. There would not be a sin anyone could commit for which we would hold him or her in condemnation, criticism or judgement.

To forgive means to accept wholeheartedly, holding no one in bondage whatever their sins; wanting no revenge and no vengeance, seeking only to embrace and serve selflessly. For where there is selflessness, there is no need for forgiveness as you and I are one. I am that — that am I. In reality there is no such thing as forgiveness. But only acceptance, 'dying daily' to a state of consciousness that accepts good and evil.

Overcoming Resistance

To cut a long story short, human evolution has been preoccupied with the fight between good versus evil. The aim of this fighting has supposedly been to preserve, promote and create a better, safer more beautiful world — in essence, to create paradise on earth. Over thousands of years, we have mastered the Way of Fighting. We have taken the brutal act of combat and developed it to the nth degree. To this day the forces of good and evil continue to fight, confront and campaign against each other. Who is actually winning? Can anyone really win? Is it necessary and if not, what other ways do we have to create a better world?

History has shown that there are four main ways to deal with opposing forces and promote social change. Each individual organisation must choose the means necessary in order to achieve the goal. The goal, whatever that is, will to a large extent determine which one of the four ways is applicable. Of the four ways, there is no better or worse, right or wrong, only the consequences of the way used.

The first is **fighting against the opposing force.** This could mean anything from a shouting match to secret campaigns to subordinate or overthrow the enemy. The use of force, be it brutal or subtle, has been the instrument used to conclude most disputes in the history of humanity. The question is, where has all that fighting and campaigning brought us? The fact is, the conditions on this earth are unbearable and are getting worse! Although fighting has been the most widely used system of social reform, isn't it possible that it has served its purpose and is now hindering progress?

The second approach to overcoming opposing forces is **non co-operation,** otherwise referred to as *"fighting without fighting"*. It is still a means of fighting but more subtle in its delivery. This system of social reform was used by Gandhi, Martin Luther King and has now become very popular in the New Age community. The fact that this method has been successfully used

during the past hundred years to bring down despots and impe-
rial tyranny is evidence that we are moving away from direct
violence as a means for promoting peace, liberty and freedom.

The third is **co-operation** as a means of promoting transformation. Where insubordination means simply not to do what is
expected or asked of us, co-operation means simply to do as we
are told. It is a conscious choice to co-operate with the 'enemy'
or the 'opposing force'. This system was used by a Buddhist monk
during the Mongol invasion of Tibet.

On hearing of the forthcoming invasion, all the monks fled
the monastery, except one monk who decided to stand still in the
middle of the huge courtyard. The invading army was led by an
infamous general on horse-back. The general rode up to the monastery, in through the gates, into the courtyard and then up to
the monk, followed by his men. The general drew his sword and
as he pointed it towards the monk he said, "Do you know who I
am?" The monk stood in silence, and the general said, "I am the
man who can thrust this sword through your heart without blinking". There was a total silence around the courtyard and then the
monk asked, "Do you know who I am?" The general remained
quiet, and the monk said, "I am the man who can let you thrust
that sword through my heart without blinking".

This approach is based on the realisation that *"I have seen the
enemy, it is us"*. To fight or be insubordinate towards another is to
oppose oneself. In consciously co-operating with those who oppose us, we eliminate the enemy within and without us.

Lastly, we come to **the way of non-resistance** whereby we
become absent from any opposing forces or systems. We are simply not there, where we may find ourselves a threat to others or
vice versa. Hence, stillness, silence, isolation and conscious suicide are the means to bring about social peace and progress. For
example, dolphins that are captured and kept in steel tanks die
within three months. Because they cannot escape, they commit
suicide — simply by holding their breath until they die. An extreme example is self-immolation which can be as powerful a

tool for social reform as secret societies or massive movements and campaigns.

The way of non-resistance as a means of social reform was used by Buddha who removed himself from the world of competition and coercion. He simply did not acknowledge the struggle and in so doing did not fuel the fire of force against force. Non-resistance is an art. When mastered, the world is yours. I can best explain its practice via a story:

A man is sitting on a wall, waving a stick and laughing frantically. He is laughing because of the screams the passers-by make as he strikes them with his stick. The secret of avoiding this collision of force would be to avoid the street altogether.

The Significance of Relating

When we meet people we have to make a choice whether to establish a relationship with them or move on. For example, choosing a partner is one of the most important decisions we can make in our lives. It is a decision that can make or break our future. Our partner's attitudes and patterns of behaviour directly influence our creativity, home and family life, financial stability and spiritual growth. "Behind every great man there is a greater woman", and vice versa. If you can make one relationship work well, i.e. the one with your partner, then the rest of your relationships will work also. Having the right partner and people around us who are compatible with what we want to do is vital in our development, be it in our personal or professional lives.

These four elements can help us choose appropriate relationships:

Method:

1. Vision

Vision

Collaboration   Communion

Commitment

Does your relationship have a vision? Are you and your partner going in the same direction? How do you feel about your partner's vision? A relationship must have a vision if it is to last and endure challenges or it becomes like a boat with two sailors paddling in opposite directions.

2. Communion

Without communion there can be no harmony, for communion means to be together or to become one. We use all forms of communication to relate to each other. The question we need to ask is whether or not there is the willingness, capacity and foundation for you to express and exchange in an honest and wholehearted manner.

3. Commitment

No matter how clear the communication and vision is in our relationships, we come upon new challenges, chaotic situations or make mistakes. This is where commitment plays a critical role in overcoming the crisis and developing the relationship into a stronger and deeper bond. Commitment means you can forgive and evolve.

4. Co-operation

A developing relationship needs continual contact and working out between partners, and although you are sure of your own aims and intentions, you will not be able to succeed without the co-operation of your partner. When two or more people work together, a process called synergy takes place, whereby the impossible becomes the possible.

Benefits

To be or not to be with a particular person or persons is a choice which will decide your future. Look back at your past and you will see how relationships have shaped your current reality. Health, wealth and empire have been laid to dust by incompatible people in the lives of kings and presidents.

As you apply these four elements and consciously choose your partner or friends, you will activate the law of attraction. You will no longer attract opposing forces, which means there will be less resistance in your life. After a while these elements will become second nature and will be used without thinking and then you will choose the best people for your future.

Making Changes

For Example

INSIGHT: I have too much grief in my relationships.

SOLUTION: I shall assess the compatibility of all my relationships via vision, communication, co-operation and commitment.

ACTION: This evening I shall contemplate on the compatibility of my relationship with . . .

INSIGHT:

SOLUTION:

ACTION:

INSIGHT:

SOLUTION:

ACTION:

INSIGHT:

SOLUTION:

ACTION:

The Way of Creating

How well does each statement describe your patterns of thought and action?

- *My creativity is guided by my inner voice.*
- *I enjoy my work for it is meaningful.*
- *I receive fair pay for what I do for my employer.*
- *I know how the creative process works and use it instinctively.*
- *I create all the wealth I need and want.*
- *I pay all my bills on time and with pleasure.*
- *I create what I want by being true and honest.*
- *I know how to turn fear into faith.*
- *I know what it feels like to plant a tree, grow a vegetable or care for an animal.*
- *I am a genius.*
- *I am devoted to using my creative genius for the benefit of all.*
- *My creativity reflects my spirituality.*
- *When I encounter my own ego or that of others, I simply do not acknowledge it.*
- *I encourage myself beyond all challenges.*
- *I empower others to new heights of creativity and responsibility.*
- *I complete my responsibilities on time or early.*
- *I know how to handle the moments of isolation and exposure which I face as a pioneer in my field of creativity.*
- *I know people who believe in me and what I want to create.*
- *I realise that my creativity is a unique contribution to my community, humanity and the earth.*
- *As I grow, I feel myself becoming a spirit of creative enterprise.*

Introduction

Each one of us is a creative genius. The genius of creating begins in creation itself. Our journey to this moment has been an epic adventure with its beginning in that flash of creation we call conception. Our creative journey in this world began by reaching the uterus, then completing the task of being born in a strange and mysterious world awaiting outside the womb. Now, our greatest challenges lie in embracing all aspects of being human and creating a role for ourselves within humanity. Each one of us is the result of the most creative act in the universe: the creation of life itself. This makes you and me the most powerful impulse in creation. Creativity is our natural birthright, so what will we do with this precious gift?

Our creativity is a channel to express our uniqueness and thus bring beauty and joy into the world. As unique individuals we have specific tasks to complete in this life, otherwise we would not have been born. The question is, what makes each one of us so unique? Is it our bodies, clothes, characters, careers, etc? Well, it's all of them rolled into one. What we say and do is a unique expression of our unique identity.

Life is a Miracle.
You are a Miracle.
Creating miracles is your birthright.

'Creating' is manifested in cooking, dancing, singing, speaking, writing, drawing, painting, inventing, teaching, etc. People use whatever they have in order to express and establish their identity and individuality in their society. It's not what they are saying that is different; it's their ways — their channels of expressing what they have to say — that are different. What each one of us is saying is, *"I need beauty in my life and I can create beauty in my life; it is not separate from me; beauty is so much a part of me that I am able to re-create it on the spot"*.

Your Creative Response

When we look at creativity in this light, it becomes not only our birthright, but also our responsibility to society. Creating is not separate from living or a part-time activity which occurs at special moments, but a moment-to-moment process. It is in every thought, emotion and action. It is your response to your inner voice which can express itself in your life in unique and personal ways. In this sense each one of us is a genius and the more geniuses the better! Each one of us has a creative level of mind which, when contacted, can reveal genius in any work undertaken. Yet, what is it exactly that makes a genius a genius?

Creative genius is the razor edge of brilliance which emanates from anyone who puts their heart and soul into what they believe. Even though one may never paint a picture, write a book, compose a musical masterpiece or create a new invention, we all have the capacity to commit ourselves to becoming a genius, creating masterpieces out of our actions no matter how ordinary they may be. Just being with friends, communicating and laughing, can give all concerned as much pleasure as may be found from sky-diving or watching a great film. This is creative genius at work.

Genius Denied

The question is, if we are all potential geniuses, why isn't the world abundant with geniuses? Where have we gone wrong? One reason for the lack of brilliance in our society is the denial of the individual's birthright of creative expression. From birth our earliest actions are brimful of creative energy. Young children are not self-conscious, and therefore have unique genius — look at their way of drawing, copied by Picasso, or recall the saying that "wisdom comes from the mouths of babies". The infant bloom of genius is soon crushed, educated out of us in preference to less individual, more conforming productivity — learning to copy rather than to originate. To deny one's creativity is to ignore the soul. People have buried their souls in favour of material consumerism.

The incessant amassing of materials has led us to bury our own creativity under a mountain of things. The media and our modern education systems conspire to mislead people, especially the young, into focusing on consumerism rather than creativity. Although our homes are full of material possessions, our hearts are often empty, our souls abandoned.

Conformity Vs Creativity

What we have created is a world of mass production, mass marketing, mass transportation, mass media and mass education. We live in a mass culture, where very often everyone looks, smells, dresses and even behaves identically. Conformity, not creativity, has become the main order in our educational and social institutions. Creativity is not considered as a natural condition of being human, but as a quirk or privilege reserved for a few eccentrics. This is why our society lacks creative genius!

Some rare individuals do escape the net of societal herding but end up suffering in isolation and turn to addiction or disappear into oblivion. The ones who do manage to blaze a trail are persecuted and put down by the people in power for disturbing the norm. So desperate is our need to maintain conformity that our lives are constantly monitored and directed by 'Big Brother', who apparently knows best and can use any means necessary to maintain control. Whether we know it or not, we have allowed our lives and passions to be controlled by a few at the top of the hierarchy — who keep telling us that we live in a free society.

Life = Work

We live in a free society, or at least we're led to believe that we do. What we call 'work' is what drives our whole hierarchical culture. Work is supposed to be a source of our livelihood, and its role is to sustain human existence, not to toil for those in position of power who live in excessive luxury whilst the exploited workers remain poor — is that work or is that slavery?

Life = Work. Every cell in your body works. Work is using energy to create. Your work and its results are central to your sense of identity and individuality. Work as we know it has become damaging to our lives. Where is the balance between life and work? With all our scientific and hi-tech know-how, why do so many toil for eight or more hours a day and still not have enough to provide food, shelter or warmth for their families? Who or what is responsible for subjecting so many to graft so hard, wrecking the lives of millions of children through child labour?

Your work is often referred to as a 'calling', like your response to your own name, it is you, it is yours, the way you make a 'living'. Having a job usually means doing someone else's work using another's tools and capital. Your integrity is gone. Life becomes split into work and re-creation, and it is in the latter that you find your selfhood again. Clearly we must rethink what work means and look at it not as a means of production or obligation, but as a passion which drives the human soul towards the creative freedom.

The Nature of Creating

The idea of discussing the nature of creating is not one that emerges within the homes, pubs and clubs of the working classes. What is paramount on the poverty-ridden streets of the world is that work — and any work — will do as long as it pays money. Work for most folk is a means to an end, which means selling their bodies, skills and, if necessary, their principles in order to ensure their livelihood. The irony is 'the end' in this scenario is spiritual suicide and Sunday is a sad day for a lot of people because Monday means going back to work. For others Monday is worse because they are out of work and on a downward spiral into the 'disposable class'. Working is the main preoccupation in all cultures world-wide. If we are to change that scenario, then we must all rethink and review what we call work and in doing so discover the true nature of creating. We begin by asking two basic questions:

What is work?
And what is not work?

What is Work?

Although there are many ways to look at work, from a 'waste of time' to 'work is worship', what we call work is what drives our whole world culture. Working is the source of our livelihood as it sustains human life. The problem is, most people, even the rich, work not because it's a passion, but because it's a compulsion. They do it not because they want to, but because they have to in order to secure a future for themselves and their families.

Security and prosperity, rather than creativity, are the main motivations in today's capitalist world culture — where the majority work against their will. The question is, if we have to work so hard simply to survive in order for a few to thrive, is this really a democracy? Is this the land of equal opportunity, liberty, and justice for all? Is this one nation indivisible under God? If not, we must ask ourselves, has work become a subtle form of slavery, and if so, is this why there is so much dis-ease between people in our society? It is important to remember the words of E. F. Schumacher who said, *"Insane work creates an insane society"*. How can we work together and not against each other?

Slavery

The point is, where does our work ethic come from and why is there so much resistance to working in all cultures around the world? Our work ethic has its roots in slavery, which was widespread in Egypt, Persia, Africa, India, China and America. Not so long ago, slavery was a natural, normal and righteous part of life. The slaves worked for their masters for food and shelter, for there was no other choice except to face the consequences.

Slavery is the taking of a person's freedom by the use of force. We think of it as something that happened long ago in another country. Then, slavery was an accepted part of life, carried out just as openly as we keep pets or run our cars today.

Those central institutions which prospered from slavery are still just as central today and use similar systems of managing people — except that now we call slavery 'work'.

Of course, there are differences between historical slavery and modern work in terms of respect, rewards and laws against physical abuse, yet there are similarities. These are hard for us to see because we have been told that slavery has been abolished, but once pointed out, they are very clear. The key point is the removal of freedom by the stronger force. In the modern workplace, that appears as exploitation of the so-called minorities.

The time, energy and skills of the best part of your life go into producing and acquiring what influential people tell you is important: money and profits, conformity, a house full of things. You do it as if you had no choice, which is as good as slavery.

The question is, does working 'for' someone, rather than 'with' them, have to mean exploitation, or a subtle form of slavery? If it does, then given the choice, most workers would flee from their employers, just like slaves ran from their masters.

Freedom

However, fleeing from our employers and our external situations is not going to lead us to freedom; that is the method we have tried and it did not work. Besides, who is going to quit their job when there is little or no hope of finding another way of earning a livelihood? The irony is, as unemployment rises, you don't have a choice about quitting, and those who are employed work even harder to hang on!

The freedom to live and lead a creative life lies not in fighting and fleeing from one's work situation, but in recognising one's own worth and vision. It is not via confrontation and revolution that the workers of the world will unite and break their chains, but via conscious evolution and transformation from 'working' to 'creating'.

The first step towards creative freedom is for each worker to ask if he or she wishes to be led by society or by their inner voice. If we lead ourselves according to our inner voice, then we are free from the bondage of work and in doing so become a self-motivated, self-determined human being able to create whatever our inner voice reveals to us.

If we give ourselves enough time to reflect and be in silence, we will hear our inner voice, clearly guiding us toward the path that is ours. However, it is not merely by listening to our inner voice alone that we come to know the true nature of creating. Inner listening is the first step which helps us to understand and unleash our awesome creative potential.

Our objective is to put this knowledge into action and transform our lives, for there are many people who are associated with wonderful teachings and therapies, yet their lives are a mess!

Why? Because they lack the know-how to bridge the gap between 'wow' and 'how'! As a young man I was constantly inspired and hyped up by pop stars, priests and politicians; yet none of them showed me a simple and effective way of creating what I wished. Time and again, inspiration turned to frustration and then addiction in order to escape the reality of my condition of paralysis. What I needed then was the means and method to put my vision into action. In effect, the Way of Creating — for what use is knowledge without action?

The Way of Creating

Creating anything for the first time, from baking a loaf of bread to flying to Mars, means going into the unknown. Creating something new is the most challenging activity, for it makes profound and extreme demands on the creator. It takes us into areas and spaces of the human experience where few have been.

In these moments of doubt and uncertainty, we need some sure way of overcoming the extreme challenges which often cause many to fall by the wayside. History is littered with men and women who had extraordinary visions and yet did not manage to come remotely close to completing their life's mission.

Everyone has at least one idea or wish in their lifetime which they wish they could make come true. But wishing by itself will not make it happen! Millions of people have wild and wonderful ideas, but these are forgotten or shelved because of the lack of creative know-how. People who do not know how to realise their dreams tend to build them up in their heads or bury them in order to make life bearable.

Those who do embark on daring adventures often waste their efforts by making unnecessary mistakes. When you make a mistake or bodge up a project, why does it happen? It is a result of not knowing the Way of Creating! In the same way, creating a fulfilling career, relationship, home or family life all begins and ends in the creative process.

The key to creating anything is contained in four fundamental steps; *clarity, creative persistence, endurance* and *completion.* In knowing how to use these steps consciously, we minimise making silly mistakes and increase the chances of completing what we set out to do. We should start by practising them on little projects and then proceed on to greater things. The sketch overleaf shows how to use the four-step process for creating anything.

Clarity is the first step on any creative adventure, for if we don't know where we are going, we will end up somewhere else!

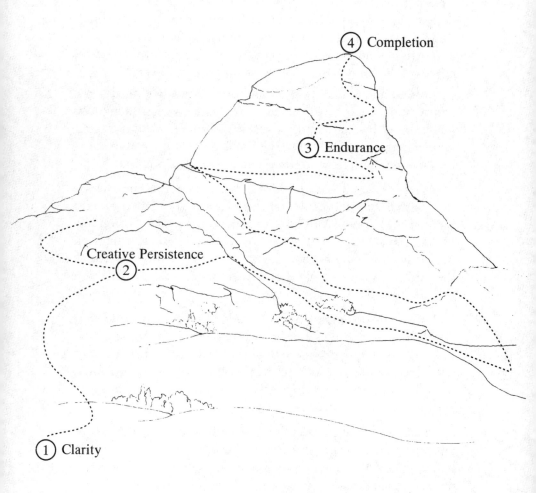

④ Completion

③ Endurance

Creative Persistence
②

① Clarity

The Four Steps of Creativity

We become clear about where we want to go by listening to our inner voice. Far too often we work on schemes and dreams which are implanted in our minds by the tabloids, the media, radio and advertising on TV. For example, how much of what we work for and buy is in accordance with our inner need? In order to regain our creative freedom, we have to listen to our own inner voice and then make our aim crystal clear before we set forth on the journey. What makes impossible visions possible is their source of inner power which is inexhaustible, and the clarity of aim on which to unleash it. We become clear about our inner aim via inner listening, contemplating on the aim and sharing the vision. The clearer the aim, the greater the chances of success.

Clarity of perception is the essential prerequisite for real evolution. Because our perception is distorted by upbringing, education and culture, our view is limited. The worst aspects of this are that we can't clearly perceive what is or what might be: this restricts creativity. The effect of this is that we find change difficult since we can't see or imagine reality being different from what its like now. We can say "I'd like to be more confident", but we can't see, or we can't create, an internal image of what being confident is like. Unless you can imagine your destination, how do you know which way to go, or even when you've arrived? Unclear perception is like living in a box, seeing life through a pinhole. Many famous, respected and influential people are only better off than the masses because their pinhole is bigger! Dismantle your box, give yourself clarity and then your creativity can be used to transform your life.

Remember the 'flies in the bottle' analogy at the beginning of this book. All you have to do is allow yourself to fly out of the other end of the bottle — to shift your perception and experience the path less travelled.

Creative perseverance is the second step, which involves finding the means and method to go forward and to overcome unforeseen challenges. No matter how carefully we may plan the journey, there are always new obstacles and opportunities we need to handle and through which we learn new things. Creative perseverance is a process of trial and error, action and reevaluation, three steps forward and two steps back. A lot of people tend to give up at this stage or start taking 'shortcuts' and sacrifice their principles.

If you stand steadfast and persevere, you will attract all the solutions, resources and people you need. Talk to someone about your situation and get new ideas or take a holiday which can help you look at things from a different angle. You need to pace yourself and use your resources wisely otherwise the next phase will be even more demanding. Try not to think of the project as being too hard, for if you think it's difficult, then it becomes difficult. Difficult does not mean the same as requiring more effort. Even simple things require effort. *"Nothing is achieved without effort. Nothing great is achieved without great effort."* Effort is the amount of your investment, a measure of the value you place on the task before you.

Endurance is the third step and perhaps the most demanding, for this is the furthest point you have been to date on your journey. Having your first child is an experience of endurance with which all mothers are familiar. Nothing can prepare you for the unknown area of childbirth and the extreme demands it will make. If there was a choice, most women would probably back out before the baby was born, right at the start of labour pains! Going through pain, strain, fear and intensity changes you: you become harder, stronger and more durable. Women athletes have increased stamina after becoming mothers. Once the goal is achieved, whether it's having a baby, or climbing Everest, the memory of the pain fades, leaving strength and learning. You could not possibly have trained for it, otherwise there would be no need for endurance! All your resources and efforts are tested to the limits and beyond. Endurance is a place and space where few venture.

As you enter this unknown, all kinds of doubts, uncertainties, insights, truths and beauty may take you into strange and altered states of being. The trick is to hang on until they pass. Do what you will to lift yourself and let go of everything which is unnecessary, or the dead weight will burn you out. There are many people who start the journey, yet only a few make it past the endurance phase; the others are either not ready or do not deserve to. The final part of the endurance phase, which I have come to call 'being there', is composed of a moment-to-moment sequence of events which is beyond time and space. You are alone and at one with everything around you, because you are focused on one thing — the goal!

Completion is the fourth and final step which most creative adventurers fail to achieve, mainly because of their fear, conditioning and lack of support. Fear — because in completing the journey they will become more comfortable and fulfilled in every aspect of their lives. Most of us are capable of handling all kinds of adversity and are familiar with suffering . But when it comes to being totally comfortable, that is the unknown which triggers off all kinds of fear, and we sabotage the final stage of completion in order to remain in the known.

Conditioning plays a very important part in completion, for if you are told that you can't do anything right, the chances are you won't. A person who has been encouraged is more confident and has more self-worth, which makes enjoying the fruits of their labour a natural right to them. Support is perhaps the most important part of the creative journey, for no matter how capable and independent we may be, no one can complete impossible challenges all by themselves. Even the thought of someone being with us in person or in spirit encourages us to persevere, endure and complete projects which are otherwise beyond our reach.

Nearing completion brings you full circle. You need to recall that clarity of creative vision which brought you on this journey, your starting point on the map from which you perceived your destination. Then, you believed it was possible; now at completion you need the touchstone of belief once more.

Bills

Bills! Why, you may ask, do I bring up the topic bills in a book on human evolution? Well, the way we pay our bills determines what we create with our lives. Although bills or payment is one of the major preoccupations in our lives, we very rarely discuss it. The issue of bills or payment, be it for services, taxes, borrowings, employment, rent, etc, almost always brings anxiety to peoples' faces. Watch the reaction of your family or colleagues when they are face to face with a bill. Why does the thought of payment evoke such anxiety, grief and fear in us? Bills have such a grip on our minds and have become so much a part of our lives that we are not aware of how much we are affected by them.

If you look closely, you will see how much of your ideas, choices, emotions and actions are influenced by how much things cost. For example, are you stuck with your job, relationship, where you live and what you eat because of your worry of not being able to afford the change?

Things could be worse you may say, but how long can you go on paying before you are simply existing to pay bills? Given the choice, would you opt out of paying bills? Would you prefer to live in a world where there is no money or payment of any form? If we went back to hunting and gathering, bartering or another system of exchange, would that free us from the bondage of payment? I think not, for there is a law of give and take which we cannot escape. We could change the means of exchanging goods and services, but the fears and phobias will still remain until we change our attitudes to giving and receiving.

A person who cannot give and receive freely is far more paranoid about payment than one who is not.

Payment is simply an act of giving.

It is not the amount that determines one's response to payment, but our attitude towards payment in general. For example, a billionaire may avoid paying taxes as much as a poor person. Most people see payment as a burden and pay for what they receive begrudgingly; even for things they need. How many times do we hear parents say "do you know how much it costs to feed, cloth and school you?" When we view anything as a burden, it becomes a burden and ultimately cripples us.

The trick is to pay with pleasure. Since we have to pay for what we receive sooner or later and whether we like it or not, we may as well pay with thanks. In which way do you view payment for the goods and services you receive, as a punishment or a privilege? Since we have to pay for everything, your answer will illustrate how miserable or pleasurable your life is.

Whether you are rich or poor, look forward to paying your bills and think how much you will enjoy the smallest things. For example, when you take your friends out for a meal, do you remember the bill or the meal? When you can take pleasure in paying, then what you are paying for becomes pleasurable.

When we start paying with pleasure, we affirm limitless wealth and abundance. A person who hates payment will attract lack and limitation. People who are always talking lack and limitation reap lack and limitation. I have heard many a 'wise man and woman' talk about creating a better world and yet cannot pay for what they want to create. Have you ever wondered why spiritual organisations and charities never have enough money to pay for their projects? Surely a truly spiritual person or organisation can create as much money or wealth as they need?

Can you imagine yourself being able to pay for creating your wildest dreams? If you can't, then you are still stuck-poor. If you can, then you are rich-free to create anything imaginable. How does it work? Payment in any form is a force which moves spirally and comes back to its creator. How you pay will determine whether you are heading for a life of lack or abundance.

The Ego

The ego is your internal entrepreneur, but it has no conscience. It can get things for you, but it's a bit of a wide boy and needs keeping in its place. Otherwise, its empire-building takes over: it gets too big and you trip over it! The ego has to have a master, not be the master. A master who won't indulge the ego's need for praise, security, attention. People with big egos are weak individuals, for the ego is a parasite which needs constant feeding to justify its size, eventually consuming its host.

Egos are like balloons: the more inflated, the more fragile they are. They're like a ghost that is present in almost every creative act. Ego interferes with the creative process from cooking for guests to classroom activities and from business meetings to the boardrooms of multinational corporations. The ego tells us that we are 'perfect', so we do not look at our own mistakes and limitations, only those of others. The inability to look at our own mistakes, limitations and failures prevents us from being creative, because we remain in the same mental space and keep repeating patterns.

The ego likes to be in total control of everything, for it wants one thing: certainty, so it can maintain its position and expand its identity. The only way it can guarantee its survival is to make sure that we succeed in everything we do. To that end it makes us plan and prepare obsessively, initiates clever conversations, negotiations, contracts and laws to ensure that what it has is protected and that it gets what it wants. Education develops the ego rather than the person, via competitive sports, exams and win-lose situations.

Whenever the ego's position or prosperity is threatened, it mobilises our intelligence, creative capacities and resources in order to fight and win. The ego wins at another's expense. This is why we have a world of winners and losers, haves and have-nots, powerful and powerless. For the ego (be it on an individual or national level), sharing anything spells danger because of the possibility of losing what the ego has worked so hard to protect.

If we look closely, all types of injustice, inequality, violence and wars are initiated by those who have the most to protect and also the biggest ego, which because of its power crushes other competing egos.

The question is, how can one remain true to one's creativity in an ego-driven, dog-eat-dog world? The solution is simple: accept failure as part of life. Create not for profit, power or fame which is what the ego wants in order to protect itself and expand. Instead, trade-in certainty for creativity, and success for satisfaction, first in 'simple' activities like cooking, cleaning, gardening, playing, making friends, etc. As this form of activity becomes daily activity, moment after moment will be filled with satisfaction until every experience is full of contentment and the need for more, bigger, better and faster will become irrelevant. This, of course, is easier said than done, for the ego begins to justify its needs and existence by mixing them with our basic needs.

The trick is not to fight the ego, for it uses confrontation and competition in order to win and make itself look great again. The simplest and easiest way to diffuse ego domination in our lives is not to acknowledge it. Do not sit with it or with those who acknowledge the ego, be it at home, school, work, the church, in government or at world summits. By focusing and feeding on our creativity, truth and beauty, good actions will manifest in all aspects of one's life — without the use of force. When the use of force is removed from our lives, we stop working for people and start working with people. This subtle but important shift transforms work into pleasure, productivity into creativity and egotism into equality in the workplace.

The Role of Courage

Creativity requires us to go above and beyond where we are or anyone has been. . . *"To boldly go where no one has gone before!"* To venture into the unknown requires an enormous amount of courage — be it taking a walk in the wood on a moonlit night, being honest, or going against the herd in your work or society. Courage helps us raise our minds and hearts above fear, conditioning and the lack of support that can kill creativity. People who lack courage often talk a lot about what they want to do or what should be done. They are the armchair philosophers who merely pay lip-service, often with a large dose of scepticism. An aged woman once told me, *"It is better to sit with a fool than with a sceptic"*!

As a young man I had always wondered how the world could be in such a mess, when there are so many wise women and men, priests and pundits. I found the answer to this dilemma when I started to launch projects that involved the co-operation of other people. We could all talk, sit, plan, prepare, until we had covered every possible angle of action. Then came the final statement: *"We can't do it because . . ."* Some of those who agreed to act and take responsibility did it from fear of ego-humiliation, and later abandoned their agreements. This process nearly killed me, as over a period of some ten years or more I poured my heart, soul and all my resources into projects which collapsed because of the lack of commitment of those around me to do what they said.

When one person abandons their commitment, the others have to carry more and one by one they leave more for others to carry, until the last one or two are burdened with crippling responsibilities. Then a man called Sanjay told me: "Never underestimate the capacity of a person to say one thing and do another". This statement changed my life!

I recognised that many people were very ambitious, but fundamentally spineless. That the contradiction between the words and the deeds was due to the lack of commitment and courage to go the distance. Now I realise that the dilemma not only exists in little groups but also within large organisations, with top people who are famous, wealthy and influential. The problem of humanity's suffering lies not in the lack of technology, materials, money or management know-how, but in the lack of courage to create a better world.

The word courage comes from a French word 'coeur', which means 'heart'. When we put our hearts and souls into a project, vision or dream, the hardest and most impossible becomes possible. This has been demonstrated by many ordinary individuals, for example: William Wilberforce, who took the responsibility to abolish slavery; Emily Pankhurst, who stood up for the liberation of women; Martin Luther King, who was the force behind equality in the USA.

Although the vision and the strategy of all great pioneers is different, what they all have in common is courage. Having courage doesn't mean you avoid fear. Fearlessness isn't courage. Courage enables you to accept your fear, rise above it and do it anyway — then, the fear ebbs away like darkness at dawn. That's what heroes get medals for!

The question is, where can I get courage from? How does a coward become courageous? The answer is as simple as in the children's story: *The Wizard of Oz*. In that story the cowardly Lion lacked courage, but he gained it by doing brave things — without realising it! If you act as if you are courageous, you will find courage, just like acting as if you are stupid makes it so. This works because the seeds of courage are in the heart of everyone: all they need is soil to grow in. That soil is challenging experiences such as the journey of creativity.

There is another difference between fearlessness and courage: in courage the risks are calculated against resources, and the courageous person is brave enough to bow out, whereas fearless people are reckless.

Creativity and Responsibility

Creativity and responsibility are two sides of the same coin. Responsibility without creativity results in a lifeless pursuit of activities which have little or no spiritual substance or satisfaction. Creativity without responsibility leaves us powerless and unable to manifest our visions and dreams. Creativity and responsibility are the yin and yang, or passive and active elements which bring truth, beauty and goodness to life. Through mastering creativity and responsibility, we realise that we have the power to influence everything and everyone around us. Only human beings seem to have the advanced awareness of creativity and responsibility to create a world living in peace and ease. This capacity can be developed in four areas of human existence:

1. **Individual**

   My creativity starts from within myself, and the first impulse starts with responding to my immediate needs. The more I nurture myself, the more creative I become.

   Creativity

   Nature

   Individual

   Humanity

   Society

   Responsibility

2. **Nature**

   The earth gave birth to us. Only living things give birth and this makes the earth a living, breathing creature. In us, this is initiated by our first breath, when we eat, drink, play in the woods, swim in the lakes and seas. In return we can plant trees, keep the rivers and seas clean, prevent scarring the earth with machines and thank the earth by being kind and affectionate to her.

3. **Society**

   There is a direct connection between the individual, creativity and society. A society that does not encourage creativity will produce citizens who are unable to take responsibility for their society. No creativity equals no responsibility equals a poor society. There are many communities, societies and states who are fiercely spiritual and yet their members cannot manifest their creativity in the physical world we live in. Ironically, some of the most religious nations to date have been unable to take care of their own citizens. If the creativity and responsibility equation is correct, then these societies, for one reason or another, are failing to release the individual's true creative potential.

4. Humanity

As we grow inwardly and outwardly so does our capacity for creativity and responsibility on ever expanding levels. Unfortunately many people never realise their ultimate vision because they are not allowed to follow their natural line of development.

In your youth you need to explore, to experiment, to risk your personal resources or identity in a new technological or social invention. Travelling into physically, emotionally, psychologically or economically unknown spaces is therefore a natural course for healthy, youthful development. In adulthood, authority and responsibility come naturally to the developing genius, innovator or pioneer. Thus the free wheeling adventurers need to come to grips with the challenges of managing money, materials, resources and people.

Whereas the twenties is a time for free-wheeling, the thirties are a prime time for focusing on structured organisation. Midlife is a time to listen to your heart first, and to your head second. As an innovator or pioneer you need to broaden your social awareness, thereby becoming a true visionary. Finally, if you have successfully undergone life transitions, as a mature individual you are ready to tap the very core of your being, your spirit of creativity. In so doing you also connect yourself with the roots of humanity.

The Significance of Creating

Every creature alive on the earth right now is creating its ideal living conditions. For example, the amoeba, one of the smallest creatures on our planet, is creating its own perfect life-sustaining conditions. Although it has no sight, hearing, taste, smell or brain, it is constantly moving to a more comfortable situation. If you were given the total freedom to create what you want, would you know what that would be and how to create it? Can you imagine what it would be like to be creatively fulfilled? If you could, would you not already be creating or living in your ideal condition?

Creating is a constant process of choice, action, condition. The aim of creating is to improve the quality of our existence. Hence, it is the example of my life working which reflects what I am creating — not how much I have achieved, amassed, or what I have produced. The simplest way to find out how creative we are is to look at our current condition, i.e. health, home, family and work. I have met many so-called geniuses, yet their current conditions are far from ideal.

What are you creating and what for? The significance of creating is to learn how to create and re-create new and better living conditions. The following method will guide you in creating a life worth living.

Method:

1. Dream

Without dreams we cannot make our dreams come true! Dreaming dreams is a way of getting in touch with our personal purpose and inner power. A dream is a vision waiting to happen.

2. **Set a goal**

   A dream is nothing other than a goal. A goal is a dream with a deadline. The moment we commit ourselves to a goal, heaven and earth move to make it happen. The trick is to plan and to put your heart and soul into the goal.

3. **Act now**

   Actions are a way of affirming a dream. The best way to embark on giant projects is to start with small steps. Completion is based on a pyramid of small actions and achievements. The key to moving mountains is to think big, and act now.

4. **Get help**

   Share your dream with other dreamers. The moment we utter the words "I have a dream", we activate the law of attraction, and everything we could possibly need and want will be given to us. All we need to do is to ask for help.

Benefits

Simple as it seems, you can use the way of creating to establish healthy foundations of living, pioneer new horizons or build empires. These principles are neutral and you can apply them to make your dream a reality. Be aware of the nature of your dream!

In daring to make you dream come true, you will never have to sit with sceptics and cynics in doom-filled living rooms, boardrooms, cafes and clubs. More importantly, you'll have a personal purpose and worth which is the ultimate wealth. And you'll have given up living a lie and you'll spend time creating what is in harmony with your inner voice. Work will then become pleasure and the rest of your life will become one long holiday. Enjoy it!

Making Changes

For Example

INSIGHT: I am aware that my fear of becoming more comfortable is preventing me from completing activities.

SOLUTION: I will start by completing the smallest actions fully.

ACTION: I shall now take one breath, deeply and completely.

INSIGHT:

SOLUTION:

ACTION:

INSIGHT:

SOLUTION:

ACTION:

INSIGHT:

SOLUTION:

ACTION:

The Way of
Being

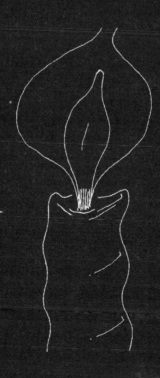

How well does each statement describe your pattern of thought and action?

- *I am free from the business whirlpool.*
- *I have an enormous bank account of good actions, so much that I have more than enough.*
- *I am living in accordance with my divine centre.*
- *I have awakened and can show others how to do so.*
- *In the midst of chaos and confusion I am centred.*
- *I know how to separate illusion from reality on the spur of the moment.*
- *I am motivated by the awareness that all-is-one.*
- *I am aware that the current world culture is based on illusion.*
- *I am aware that complexity is bondage and that simplicity is freedom.*
- *I live a simple life — look!*
- *I can transform my pain and pleasure into paradise.*
- *I am guided by my intuition.*
- *I am always in the right place at the right time.*
- *I am completely harmless, for I am free of fear and guilt.*
- *I do not need faith from the scriptures or sermons because I have natural faith.*
- *As I stand naked in the woods or at home, I feel completely safe and supported by other people and the earth.*
- *I devote the rest of my life to serving humanity and the earth.*
- *I can create miracles without possessions, power or position.*
- *The greatest gift I have given to my family and friends is the example of my own life working.*
- *I constantly live in a state of peace and ease —in 'being' , itself.*

Introduction

Being, or shall I say the quality of being, is the most important part of H.E.L.P. because the condition of being determines how we feel and what we focus on. It has a direct effect on our external environment, such as home, family, society and nature. Hence, improving the quality of life to the point of well-being is the goal or essence of this programme and this chapter. However, before we explore how to reach a state of well-being, it is vital that we understand what has caused the lack of well-being in the first place. Many of us often experience a momentary sense of well-being, but tend to become busy and disorientated with other things.

The world we live in is busy, and being busy is what denies us the right of being human. We are all busy bodies! We are busy being busy, rather than being human. If we look at any creature, a cat for example, it does what is necessary and no more. A cat is a cat, a dog is a dog, and a dolphin is a dolphin. Yet, humans try to be more than they are and in so doing become busy. The busier we become the more we neglect and sacrifice being human itself.

How many people do you know who are not busy?

From a very early age we are encouraged to be busy and business-like. Being busy implies success, greatness, happiness — and the busier you are the more you are in demand and the more people look up to you! Everyone — from primary school teachers to the presidents of our nations — are all busy!

Being busy is not necessarily a physical activity, but more a sense of hurriedness. Even people who are bored can be mentally busy trying to escape the reality of their condition. For example, a workaholic may be busy working, while an alcoholic may be busy drinking. Being busy is a very diverse phenomenon: it can appear in many activities from wanting to make more money or material things to meditation. In one's desire to be creative, it is easy to become busy — the secret is to take the time to rest after activity. Do your best and rest. The inability to rest makes us treat ourselves wickedly: *"There is no rest for the wicked"*!

Beware of working with people who have busy lifestyles, as unless you have the capacity to hover and land at will, you can get sucked into the business world whirlpool. Once in the whirlpool, we become speed-freaks hooked on our own adrenaline and feel excitement as we go round at the top end, for it beats boredom hands down. Being busy initially gives us a buzz, which we get addicted to. In due course we become disorientated as we get sucked into the inertia of the whirlpool and end up going nowhere fast.

At this point we are poised to ask the questions, *"Am I in the whirlpool and if so, what can I do about it? How can I find lasting and real fulfilment whilst continuing to be effective in the world?"*

In order to get out of the whirlpool, we first have to know the cause of the force: and then learn the ways and means to become free of it. To begin with, let's look at the cause by imagining the whole world culture as a global game show. We all participate in the game via books, magazines, movies, education, religion and especially television. In the United States for example, 99.5% of homes have television sets and on average, the TV is on for eight hours per day. Electronically, the entire country is wired together as a single entity. The problem, however, is not the television, for the whirlpool which is causing the swirling mass of busy humanity was set in motion long before the advent of television. The cause is not the medium or media, but the subliminal message coming from the television, which propels the global game show. But what is that?

The vision is of paradise, and profit, production, power and position that are the means of attaining the money and material objects necessary for its success. Paradise is the global aim and we all want to achieve it, because it is in our nature to live in that state of absolute bliss. The problem is that the paradise being peddled by the media is an illusory one, and doesn't actually bring fulfilment at all, but more wanting and non-fulfilment. If we really did not play the game, we'd not strive for success, greatness, happiness and righteousness, as we have these already!

The source of the vision lies in our pain, which motivates us to strive for pleasure. Since birth, we have been striving after pleasurable pursuits, which now run into thousands of thoughts and activities which make us busy. The global game show is perpetuated by the interplay between pain and pleasure. The goal is paradise.

The only way to stop the buck is to ask the question, *"Am I busy or not?"* Are we without a thought of busi-ness in our minds? Failing that, can we find hurriedness, the symptoms caused by being busy at home, at work, in the car or in the office, at church or at the social club? Hurriedness is a symptom that brings the reality of our lives to the forefront. We can see it in ourselves, each other, in the media and in every aspect of our society and world culture where the game is played.

The irony is, even those amongst us who are supposed to be more spiritually advanced are often busy bodies and use the excuse of wanting to serve humanity as a justification. We must realise that even the busi-ness of serving humanity is a betrayal of one's being human and an act of genocide when viewed on a grander scale.

The funny thing is, in working closely with both commercial and charitable organisations at the highest levels, I observed that in charities, there were far more key individuals burned out on the track. Yet, the CEO's of the commercial organisations, with all their greed and ignorance, had worked out that *results come from doing the right thing, not from doing things right.*

When we look back through history, we can see that the greatest reforms and legacies of goodwill were manifested by those who were not being busy, but simply being human. They had understood that results come not from being busy and not from being seen to be doing many things, but from doing a few things.

Like everyone else I too was caught up in the swirling mass of humanity for many years. I became very busy, teaching, talking, meditating, flying . . . Until I was burned out. Then, I took a vow that I would never be busy again. The irony is, I can get much more done now than when I was being a busy body. It seems to me that the more I want to do, the quieter I must become; the more I want to establish, the less I must possess; the more I need to accomplish, the less I need to do. As this awareness unfolds, I find myself doing less and spending most of my time doing nothing, saying nothing, just being . . . Being itself.

The Nature of Being

The earth is crawling with billions upon billions of life-forms, of which humanity is one species and you are one human being. Every time you and I breathe, we consciously or unconsciously affirm our natural right to live. At this moment an infinite number of creatures are breathing in and out. This makes the earth a living, breathing creature suspended in space. Just like any other creature it has its own identity and beauty. We all know that the earth is beautiful seen from outer space. Yet what makes it so appealing is the aggregate activities and contributions made by each grain of sand, drop of water, leaf, insect, bird, animal and you! So the next time you stand in awe of the earth's beauty from space, remember your part in the scheme of things. That without you, this earth would not be so appealing and that your presence and participation is vital to its continuation.

If we view the earth as a playground, then we are all players playing our part in order to learn and live out our own destiny. As in any game, no one individual or creature is more important than another, for without each one the team would be incomplete. This makes our individual participation and contribution vital to the well-being of the earth and all its inhabitants. You are the most important person in the world, for what you do can make or break this earth. For example, you can plant one acorn from which will grow millions and millions of trees. Or you can light the match that can burn millions and millions of trees, leaving scars on the earth that could be seen from space. This makes what we decide to do as individuals a matter of grave concern, for the earth is currently being killed by our actions.

Almost everyone is aware of the distressful condition of the earth. Yet, most people think it's impossible to stop the destruction. Why? Could it be that we are looking in the wrong place for the solutions? How many of us, in the history of humanity, have set out to create a better world? An endless number of organisations have made their contributions towards 'getting there'. Every conceivable strategy and means have been tried over the past six thousand years and yet, with all due respect, we have not 'arrived'. Where has all that action brought us?

The fact is, the earth is dying faster than ever before and may soon enter into inertia, from which it may never recover. Have we misunderstood the problem and are merely applying the wrong solution in the wrong place? If that is true, then what is the problem and how do we find the solution to a problem we don't yet know?

Well, the first thing we need to understand is that the secret of solving impossible puzzles is to try impossible solutions! Where do we find impossible solutions and if we do, how can we diffuse impossible solutions into the world culture? At this point we can give up and die, or try something new. For those who say we have no chance, I say we take it anyway. If we have no chance, what is there to lose?

To begin with, we have to understand that the impossible is often the untried, and thus, such a solution may bring forth resistance and ridicule. I put forward 'being' itself as the main solution to the salvation of our souls and the earth. Why? Well, so far we have tried everything from the crusades to massive campaigns to save the world! Even the experts are now beginning to realise that time is running out and soon it will be too late! We must come to realise that we have been committing suicide step by step. We need simply to stop and take stock of our own well-being. Even our efforts to change the world must take second place. We must realise that the secret to solving personal and planetary problems lies in our own well-being. It is a myth that such transformation is slow in its effects, and it stays a myth because no one's ever done it on a large scale.

Of course, 'being' as a method for transformation seems very slow when compared to the modern day methods of massive organisations and their campaigning capacity. Yet if we look at the outstanding reformers in history, the greatest gifts they gave were the examples of their lives. In effect the quality of their being, which gave power and purpose to their actions, left legacies for future generations.

The one thing they all had in common was the condition of their well-being. 'Being' itself — being, is simply existing in the moment. It is life as it is. You know what it feels like because you felt it as a baby. This can be explained by a simple analogy: A rose is a rose is a rose; Krishna is Krishna is Krishna; Buddha is Buddha is Buddha; Jesus is Jesus is Jesus; Mohammad is Mohammad is Mohammad and so on. They lived their lives unhurriedly, simply being and in so doing brought about goodness around them, often without any action at all.

The nature of being it seems is the easiest and simplest thing to discover, for it requires not doing, but being. We find it hard because we apply 'doing' to solve all our problems which in turn creates even more problems. We have become 'human doings' and need to be 'human beings', if we are to survive and evolve to the next phase of our evolutionary journey. Being is simple, and it would be a shame if we complicated it. The earth is simply being; it does not try to change us, judge us or punish us and yet all the truth, goodness and beauty we know has come from it. Surely by now our common sense is telling us that the cause of our suffering is due to the denial of our being and the solution for the transformation and the salvation of humanity lies in the nature of being.

The Way of Being

No one can explain what being is, for it is a state in which speech falls away. What we can explore and develop is the Way to Being, by acknowledging its actual existence. In our 'busi-ness' to get to wherever we want to be, we have denied or become blind to a part of human nature we call 'being'. This aspect of our nature is out of focus or out of sight, thus it very rarely comes up in conversation.

The question is, how can we get in touch with that part of us that we don't even know exists, let alone live in that state? We shall rediscover and live in our own being by the use of analogies and then by a process of choosing 'either/or' in the world of illusion and reality.

We start by coming to terms with the idea that our lives have become a babble of thoughts and hurried actions. Generation after generation have focused on the material and mental development of our culture: humanity as a whole has become blinded by narrow vision. It's as though the mind of humanity has been blinkered like a racehorse and we do not have access to all-round vision. The following simple experiment will, in part, demonstrate what I am trying to explain and add valuable insight into the process.

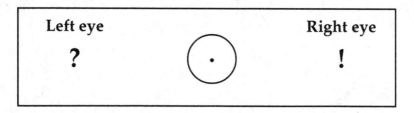

The blind spot of the eyes. Hold the book four to five inches from the face. Shut one eye and fix the other one on the dot. As you move your head from side to side ,the question mark or the exclamation mark will appear and disappear.

The nature of our being lies in the blind spot of our awareness; we know that such a blind spot exists, for sometimes we have seen 'sparks' coming out of it and in rare moments we can see it head on. In theory, all this makes sense, but so have so many speculations on the notion of being in the history of humanity! The question still remains as to where this place exists and how we can find it.

How can we see through the fog of tradition, confusion and illusion which has prevented us from finding our way to being?

To begin with, we need to acknowledge that being is a part of our daily lives and not some far-out experience reserved for the privileged few. Secondly, we must realise that we can live in our own being simply by making decisions and choices which enhance the quality and conditions of our lives. Life's equation is very simple: if I make bad decisions, I suffer the consequences; and with every good decision I make, I become more comfortable. Hence, how I feel now is the result of a long line of decisions I have made in the past. Of course, our decisions and daily lives are influenced by our upbringing and surroundings, but once we know the pitfalls we can avoid falling arse over face by consciously choosing the most appropriate course of direction.

However, to make such wise decisions on life, we need the wisdom of what is true or false, illusion or reality . . . This wisdom takes a lifetime to develop — or so we're told! The dilemma is, if the wisdom to separate illusion and reality takes a lifetime and special circumstances to develop, what use is it to anyone — especially the young and ordinary folk on the street?

This scenario brings us back to rely on our common sense and resolve the problem by using everyday knowledge. What we need is a simple method or process which can help us separate truth from falsehood and illusion from reality on the spur of the moment, for that is how life's decisions are made. The following process is so simple and effective that it makes our perception razor sharp and can be used by ordinary folk on the street. We begin by building on the notion that the world is composed of opposites: night and day, front and back, inside and outside etc. Illusion and reality are also opposites and exist simultaneously within and without us. Knowing which one is illusion or reality is the key to making the choices that create pain, pleasure or paradise. From what I can gather, the whole world is motivated by either illusions or reality. The following five illusions and realities can be seen as the source of opposing forces which play a part in the evolution of our species. By making choices to follow either illusion or reality, we can learn from their consequences and adapt our decisions according to what we know. The following diagram will help refine the choice process in the lives of ordinary individuals.

ILLUSION	REALITY
Gain and Loss	Neutrality
Success and Failure	Contentment
Great and Small	I am that I am
Right and Wrong	Discretion
Heaven and Hell	Now

Fundamentals of separating illusions from reality

This process will awaken people. People are asleep in the Adamic dream of opposites. Lack, loss, failure, sin, sickness and death are seen as realities. The story of Adam is that he ate of the fruit of illusion and fell into a deep sleep. In this deep sleep he vainly imagined good and evil. In doing so he invented the opposites in his mind. He created the reasoning mind, which has come to dominate all our choices throughout the ages. Of course, Adam stands for the Generic Mind. The story of the garden of Eden portrays paradise — reality perceived by the superconscious, where whatever we need and want is always at hand. With the development of the reasoning mind, we have reasoned ourselves into lack, loss, limitation and failure. Over generations, we have learned how to earn our bread by the sweat of our brow, instead of *being* divinely provided for. The time has come to free ourselves of the illusion and re-create the garden of Eden. The following five steps will intuitively guide you to reconnect with reality. *"All that the kingdom can afford is yours."*

Neutrality is the first step we must take toward the discovery of reality. Everything in and around us is moving, and whenever there is movement, there is change. Heracleitus said, *"One can never step in the same river twice"*. Life is like a river and the more we flow with it, the less we suffer. We suffer because we get stuck on its banks or try to stop its flow. When we flow, we can change with change, constantly — not by anticipating, but as it happens. We tend to think that if we let go and flow, we will lose what we have gained, ie money, material things, land . . .

Our society views life in terms of profit and loss. The way we view life forms our reality. The current world culture is based on the idea of gain and loss. Although there is enough for everyone, gain, greed and desire outweigh what we actually need. Greed is born of the fear of not having enough. The irony is, what we fear most is what happens to us. If one yearns for gain, then loss becomes the enemy within. The fear of loss drives people to compete against each other. Individuals who are competitive are motivated by fear — be they 'winners' or 'losers'. Fear breeds fear and makes us hold on — fixed. We close down and cocoon ourselves.

Yet, life is changing all around us. Everything we need and want is all around us, but in a fixed state we cannot give or receive. This is why millions of people are suffering and (indirectly) starving.

Every passing moment, billions of people make decisions based on the illusion of gain and loss. Their decisions result in fierce competition — a deadly virus which is destroying humanity. Ironically, the cure for this disease costs nothing, for we were born with it — neutrality. Neutrality is the ability to view change as a neutral event. To be free of the illusion of gain and loss, one has to become neutral towards the events of the world. This neutrality is expressed in the form of a 'loving judge', witnessing the drama of gain and loss. Some are winning a lottery, losing a fortune, inheriting land and property, cheating in business, being sent to prison or being put in a position of power. In the seesaw of society, the judge remains neutral, flowing and changing, and has nothing to do with gain and loss.

Contentment is the second step towards living in realisation. Contentment is the natural state of every living thing, for having done its daily chores, it returns to a state of rest and relaxation. Beauty is a relaxed human being who is content, and that is why babies are so appealing. Adults, however, having all they need and wanting still, cannot be content, and yearn for more, in the belief that there is never enough. This yearning for more is propelled by the subconscious fear that life does not support us and to survive we must have more, more and more.

Consequently, our society and the whole world culture is based on success and failure which feeds itself on the hierarchy of winners and losers — of which you are one. Our society idolises winners, and success is the place to be; losers are failures to be rejected on the scrap heap of disposable people. Ironically sooner or later everyone fails, for success is nothing other than a postponement of failure. Besides, if success is such a great place to be, when we look at the successful individuals today and in history, we must ask ourselves, do we want to end up like them?

Success and failure are like a mirage, and mirages can never be reached, whereas contentment is always present in all circumstances. The trick is to realise that every time we make a decision motivated by success or failure, we sow the seeds of suffering. When we see ourselves suffering, all we need to do is stop competing and be content with what we have and who we are. Even in the most dire situations, we can find something to be grateful about and in being contented we unleash the power and beauty of being human.

Be still for a moment and ask yourself what is missing from your life, and how you can get it. The secret of contentment is a state of mind, not an action, possession or a place in the future. The moment we stop yearning, contentment will be upon us.

I am that I am is the third realisation towards awakening, for the moment we acknowledge that we are all the same under the skin, we become equal. Yes, we are all born equal, and at birth we have no more or less respect for our parents than we do for pop stars, politicians, pundits and priests. When we were infants, we just knew we could achieve anything without a thought of not being good enough or becoming great. This self-confidence or self-worth was then washed away by the continuous pounding of the status-driven culture we live in. This is why most ordinary individuals believe they are simply too small or sheep like to make a significant contribution to humanity. The analogy of the sheep and shepherd has been abused by our leaders to maintain control over the masses and protect their own position and prosperity. We need to realise that great and small are relative, for who is Napoleon without his army; or who is the Pope without his cardinals; who is the President without his political allies?

When I used to teach at our training centre in Germany, people used to come from all over the world to learn and pay homage. From my room I could see an aged woman tending her garden, moving so slowly and peacefully. Her name is Mrs Elmshodt, but her name does not appear on any Global Gurus List – yet her quiet application to her work was most inspiring and helpful to me.

When we look at the true leaders in the history of humanity, we can see that they did not need to demonstrate their greatness by elevating themselves above the common folk or by surrounding themselves with pomp and grandeur.

In order for us to be free from the tyranny of great and small, we must beware of the "Emperor's new clothes" and not bow to images or individuals because everyone else is. The next time you feel daunted by life or larger-than-life people, remember that you are no less or more than they are . . . I am that I am.

Discretion is the fourth step on the journey of self-realisation. Life is not a chance! It's a choice and sooner or later we need to make difficult decisions which can have lasting consequences on the rest of our lives. As we make decisions, we need to use our own discretion based on what is good for us and not what is right or wrong in the eyes of our culture. Making decisions based on our own discretion will set us free from the bondage of tradition and blaze a trail into the unknown. In other words, if we use discretion to make our life's decisions, we become masters of our own destiny. We come to realise that the right and wrong ways of doing things are rules made by the rulers who did not consult us and are not necessarily valid for today's environment.

The majority of today's discoveries have been brought about by individuals who did not compare themselves with others or care what was the right or wrong thing to do. Galileo proclaimed that the earth was not the centre of the universe, from observations made through his telescope. At the time, this was blasphemous, and he spent many years of his life in hiding. History has shown us that what was once believed to be wrong has often turned out to be the best way! Of course there are those amongst us who will proclaim that doing what is right is right and living righteously is the best way to live. This may be true, but the question is, what is causing all the suffering in our life, if we are already living righteously?

The bottom line is that rising above what is believed to be right or wrong does not mean we can be irresponsible; just as doing what is thought right doesn't guarantee that we're being responsible. Questioning what we believe to be right or wrong can be very unnerving, for it leaves us with what is now. We can no longer rely on other people's beliefs, but have to develop our own ideas and use our own discretion to make decisions.

Now we take the fifth and final step towards self-realisation. The moment is now. In this moment, this 'now', we have the opportunity to escape or enter into the divinity of our being. But is it beyond our immediate capacity to do that at this moment, or even later on tonight? We shall discover in this nowness that we are again face to face with the opportunity to escape. If we are not prepared to enter it now, there will be tomorrow, next week or next year. Each time that opportunity for total realisation comes to our thought, it will be now. A thousand years from now, it will be the eternal now to us.

Now is always the time to enter into our being, but while that 'now' may come to us at this moment, to some it may have come years ago and to others it may come years hence. Whether or not it comes at this moment or in the future, it will always be now. Each one of us has to face every moment of every day with this ultimate reality we call now . . . Look we are here now!

How can we not waste these precious moments and use every opportunity to live in our being? Believe it or not, by having taken the first four steps, we are now very close to entering the state of being. Now, let go of the illusion of heaven and hell, good and evil, for there is no such place or thing. The chase for heaven is what has caused us to be one step away from being. Believe it or not, we have become busy trying to get from here to heaven.

Heaven is not a place: it is a state of being.

Be aware that you are here now and that this moment now is your only reality. Everything in the universe exists now within and without you. At this moment of being, we are beyond the duality of 'either/or' and everything just is; every moment does not have to have a purpose or meaning. "I am, it is, you are". This is total realisation.

What is Wisdom?

In knowing the difference between illusion and reality we gain valuable insights into the nature of living things. In effect we become the master of opposites, for duality no longer determines our decisions. We see things the way they are and do not allow our body, mind and emotions to become caught up in them. We start to glide rather than grind our way through life, thus avoiding chaos with other people. In so doing, we take the way of least resistance which enables us to get things done easily and quietly. Indeed, real power is when we put knowledge into action and change the face of events.

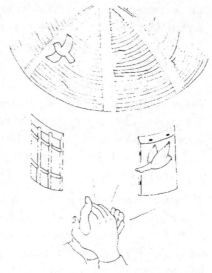

Wisdom leads to freedom and a wise person knows how to set people free. For example, a Sufi master claps his hands on seeing frightened birds trapped in a mosque so that they may fly out the window.

True wisdom is knowing how to use power. There are many who possess the knowledge and power to influence the course of events world-wide, and yet use their influence for personal greed and glory. Wisdom is measured in one's capacity to take responsibility and to care for others, not the ability to control people in order to protect one's power and position. For example, when we look at the lives of the saints, sages and prophets in human history, we can observe they possessed little or no personal wealth. It was not what they possessed; i.e. profound words, money, material wealth, power or fame that enabled them to change history, but the way they treated people and responded to circumstances. The way they lived. The quality of their being.

Pain, Pleasure and Paradise

For most of us life began with screams of pain from our mother, then a slap on the bottom to make us cry, the first burning breath of dry air in our lungs, followed by bright lights, loud noises. We were then wrapped in towels which felt like sand paper next to our hypersensitive skin. Pain was the first introduction to our lives and now these initial layers of memory are thought to govern our every action and reaction today.

Our lives are still affected by pain and we spend a lot of time and energy trying to manage pain or painful experiences, be they physical, emotional or mental. Clearly, we need to retain the ability to feel pain, for without it we would not know when things are hurting us. The question is, how much pain do we need to feel in order to be happy, healthy human beings? Can we have too much pain and become addicted to it just as we do with other stimulating activities such as eating, drinking, running, meditating, etc?

The truth is, pain leads to suffering, which may sometimes be necessary for us to learn lessons, even for the salvation of humanity, but has the pain and suffering become so normalised that it is now leaving behind diseased and deranged human beings? To use one extreme example, torture is an excessive form of pain and suffering which has crippling consequences on the individual. If this is true, how does the idea and practise of universal suffering promote individual well-being? Despite all the pain and suffering in human history, why is humanity still hell-bent on destroying itself and the earth? Is it possible that the majority of the human population is addicted to pain and that is why we keep re-creating so much suffering in different and diverse situations?

A brief look at the news will reveal our preoccupation with spreading information on pain, violence, disease and suffering as many times a day as it is possible! Pleasure is the opposite reaction to pain, and to feel pleasure we will use all kinds of addictions as tools to treat the wounds and scars left behind by the pain. The equation is simple: the more pain in one's life, the greater the need for pleasurable fixes so we can prepare ourselves for the next bout of suffering. The strange thing is, pleasure is a fleeting moment, whilst suffering lasts much longer! So, pain is the main addictive drug of humanity, which is freely available to all ages and races around the world. Then, to ease the pain we are offered the chance of happiness via fancy clothes and cosmetics, diamonds and drugs, material objects and medals, power, prosperity and position in society.

For thousands of years we have been offered all kinds of possibilities and panaceas of happiness and paradise if we simply buy or practise what we're told. Yet the majority of people still face suffering and hardship in their struggle to attain paradise on earth. We need to re-examine the method and process which could lead to paradise, and perhaps redefine the meaning of paradise itself. Paradise in most cultures has come to mean perfection in every sense of the word. But, is perfection really possible? In fact, paradise is in the eyes of the beholder. It has nothing to do with perfection or the striving for paradise via spiritual teachings or therapies.

Paradise is the condition of the perception of one's life in a state of contentment. Of course, there is still some degree of pain and suffering in that condition of personal paradise. For example, when one steps in dog shit or stumbles on a pebble, does that mean paradise disappears? To live in paradise is simpler than we are led to believe, for all we need to do is to begin appreciating what we have and at once paradise will manifest in one's life. For example, there was a time in my life when I was being shot at — I managed to escape with my life. Very soon after that, I realised that paradise is here and now, in every moment, because no one is shooting at me! Since that realisation I have lived with a sense of paradise and everyday I find new and exciting reasons why my life is paradise. Adjusting your threshold will present new opportunities to experience paradise.

Once we experience a personal paradise, we cease to be motivated by pain or pleasure which are temporal, because paradise is a constant state of contentment. Some would argue that constant contentment would make us apathetic or inactive. I have found the reverse to be the case. I am now more caring, conscious and creative than ever before. For me, pain and pleasure are lessons I had to learn, like removing my hand from the fire. Having learned the lesson, we do not need to keep repeating it, but need to teach it to others. The message is: beware of the traps and trappings which lead to pain and pleasure. In order to live in paradise we need to be patient and appreciate whatever we have in the moment.

The Role of Simplicity

Simplicity is freedom. Simplicity brings joy and balance, whereas duplicity brings greed, anxiety and fear. Simplicity is an inward reality that results in an outward lifestyle. Both inward and outward aspects of simplicity are essential for well-being. We deceive ourselves if we believe we can possess the inward reality without it having a profound effect on how we live. To attempt to arrange an outward lifestyle of simplicity without the inward reality, leads to deadly confusion and panic. Reality begins with inward simplicity and unity. It means to live from the centre of our being.

Experiencing inward simplicity liberates us outwardly. Speech becomes truthful and honest. The lust for status and position is gone, because we do not need status and position to live in the divine centre. Because we lack the divine centre, our need for security has led us into an insane attachment to things. Inwardly, we are fractured and fragmented, trapped in the maze of competing attachments. One moment we make decisions on the basis of realisation and the next moment out of fear of what others will think of us, or out of illusion . Humanity has no unity or focus concerning the orientation of our lives. Contemporary culture lacks both the inward realisation and the outward lifestyle of simplicity.

We must clearly understand that the lust for affluence is psychotic because it has completely lost touch with reality. We crave for things we neither need nor enjoy. We are made to feel ashamed to wear the same clothes or to use objects until they are worn out. The mass media has convinced us that to be out of step with fashion is to be out of step with reality. It is time we awaken to the fact that to be healthy in a sick society means that sick people think you are sick! Simplicity is the solution to our sick society. Although I cannot describe all the inner ways of experiencing simplicity, I would like to mention ten ideas for the outward expression of simplicity. They should not be viewed as laws but as one attempt to flush out the misunderstanding of simplicity in twenty-first century life.

- Buy things for their usefulness rather than their status.
- Reject anything that is producing an addiction in you.
- Develop the habit of giving things away.
- Throw away or sell off everything you have not used for five years.
- Learn to enjoy things without owning them.
- Develop a deeper appreciation for creation. Get close to the earth.
- Avoid buying too much food, drink, clothing, etc.
- Use plain and honest speech: let what you say be simply "yes" or "no".
- Reject anything that will breed oppression in others.
- Shun whatever would distract you from your main goal.

Live simply
so that others may simply live.

Fear and Faith

Over ninety-five per cent of our behaviour is a repetition of yesterday. That may be fine if you are happy, but what if you're suffering? What is it that makes us repeat the same patterns of behaviour day after day, decade after decade, generation after generation? There are many reasons, but they all stem from one source — FEAR. Fear of what? Fear of CHANGE. Why change? Well, change by its very nature means going into the unknown. We fear the future because we do not know what will happen to us. Change is going to occur between now and then. We cannot control what has not happened yet and that uncertainty leads to hesitancy, anxiety, and fear.

The understanding of fear and faith is relevant to becoming a total human 'being'. We have seen that change evokes fear within us. We cannot escape change, because change is forever present in the universe. However, 'being' is the only part of our nature which does not change. In that state of being there is no fear; because there is no change. But how do we get to that state of being? Its very simple, by having FAITH. As we saw earlier, it is doubt which leads to fear and faithlessness.

Almost everything we do, say and think is either motivated by fear or faith. We think over seventy thousand thoughts a day. Even the thought of holding someone's hand at work evokes fear in us. Try this simple exercise:

Close your eyes and hold your arms wide apart, pointing your index fingers outward. The aim is to bring the tips of the index fingers to touch at a point in front of you.

Whether you made contact or missed is not the issue. The question is: was there the slightest of doubt? That doubt contains fear. The world we live in is rampant with such fear — success and failure, profit and loss, even life and death. Yet, how do we move from a life of fear to one of faith, when most people around us are motivated by fear?

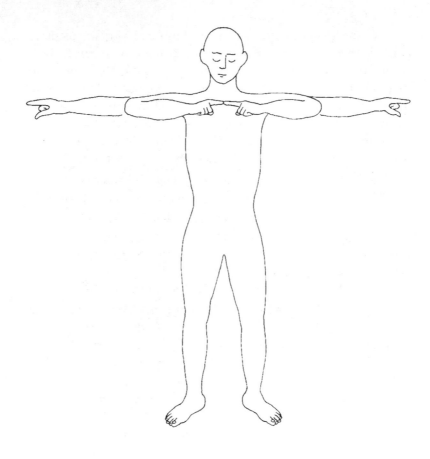

No one can give you faith; you cannot get it from reading the scriptures or sermons. Faith can only be demonstrated. There is no such thing as blind faith. Faith is anything but blind. To gain faith one must be ready to see it, not with our intellect or eyes, but with our insight, which is seeing with our mind's eye.

The oak tree grows slowly and naturally;
it grows from silent and unseen roots.

The fear that exists within and without us has made us blind to the faith we once had. For example, a new born creature, be it animal or human, has little or no fear of anything or anyone. It naturally believes that the world is a safe place to 'be' in. That 'being' is the same in every living thing. Faith is therefore inherent to a human being. The baby does not fear because it is still living in that state of being — natural faith. Because it has no fear, it does not need faith to overcome it.

The way to regain that condition of being is by simply believing that you have faith — not in anything or anyone but yourself.

Before you were conceived, you completed a journey of swimming the equivalent of a thousand miles. You did the seemingly impossible. Compare what you want to do today with that achievement. Take notice of how you feel and think — you are here, now. Make an affirmation: *"I believe in me"*.

Believing in yourself is the step that leads from fear to faith. By having faith in yourself, you will have faith in your work, vision, and the future. Fearless faith will lead to non-resistance to change. When we stop resisting change, we live in the moment without fear of the next. This state of bliss, joy and love is called being. That's when a truly daring adventure will begin.

The Aim

At one time I was in a company of soldiers at war. My life, to all senses and circumstance was very near death. I felt totally lost in the chaos and carnage all around me. Life and death had become insignificant as no one, it seemed, had any control over what was happening or who was going to live or die. I could not work out who I was, where I was, what was happening and why I was alive! Nothing seemed to matter in those timeless moments, as if life and death meant nothing and were not important in the first place. Yet, in the middle of all this there was a part of me that had remained unaffected by the whole aimlessness, by the whole sequence of events. Somehow I stood perfectly still and this part of me whispered, *"Being . . . Being itself"*. In those moments I realised that being was the purpose of my life. The following words are a clumsy attempt to share some reflections based on that experience.

For me the purpose of my life is to live out my life unhurriedly. Life is not something we can chase, for the chase takes us away from life. For example, if we try to chase being via meditation, mantras or prayer, they are a means to an end! Now, being is the 'end', which is right here anyway, so all we need to do is stop trying — and that's being! You see, as we chase this or that, we think about what we chase; we think about 'it', which is always one step away from where we are. But being is right here, it's not that or over there where we are trying to be — it's here. The secret is to simply stop as though we have arrived at a destination called being. Stop trying and trust that you have reached the point of being — the Goal. Stop doubting for the slightest doubt can send us on the journey again! This is why it is said that the discovery of the soul is the hardest journey we can undertake.

Being is the easiest for it requires us to be effortless. Be still, for life cannot be fetched! This is how it works; somewhere in our mind's eye there is a memory which knows the place of being. Just like a Zen archer can take aim, shoot the arrow and hit the target with his eyes closed, we too can remember the point of being before we lost aim. This is why being still, in my experience, is the fastest way to being! Stillness is faster than light, thought or spirit. Being is a state of nothing or nothingness and stillness is as close to nothingness as we can be. Ironically, being requires us to become the aim, for when we aim at a target we become separate from it. We use effort to get from here to the target, and some even get lost on the way. The funny thing is, all the effort, energy and explanation on finding one's being is unnecessary if we can only see the folly of the journey! The journey, we must realise, is merely a diversion or delay, a substitute for the real thing. We believe that being is something spiritually sublime and beyond the reach of ordinary mortals. The truth is, it is easy and rooted in our daily lives.

Try This:

Have a bath in warm water. Close your eyes and let the warmth of the water soak away all your thoughts and feelings about the past and future. Listen to your breath rising and falling. You are here in eternity — the external womb.

The Significance of Being

Being simply means living naturally — without guilt or obligation. The next time you watch a wildlife documentary observe how the animals behave. Even in front of the camera, they eat, shit, sleep and have sex freely. Deep down inside we want to live freely and without guilt. What prevents us from doing so is the use of force.

We force our bodies to behave and work in ways they do not like. We force our minds to learn and live according to expectations rather than to what is natural. We suppress our emotions and deny our feelings. We force ourselves to live a lie and make believe it is us. The use of force prevents anything from behaving naturally — freely. When anything is forced, it eventually becomes damaged or breaks. Is it any wonder that there are so many people with broken lives? Mending broken lives is like assembling a jigsaw. An infant school teacher gave a child a torn image of the earth to assemble. Within a few minutes, the child brought back the complete picture. Unbeknown to the teacher, there was a diagram of a human being on the back page, which the child had used instinctively.

In the same way, once we know the significance of being, instinctively, we assemble and nurture ourselves to a state of total well-being. The process below shows how we can begin to free ourselves by becoming aware of our real needs and wants.

Method:

Body

The body is a great place to start, because the body does not lie. We are often untrue with our minds and emotions, but the body we can see. What we see is a reflection of what is happening inside and in the past. By looking at our body we can find out what we need to nurture.

Mind

The mind is like a chariot of the body and its five senses are its horses. The mind is the chooser of the direction and experience. How we think right now is a direct result of the choices we made this morning, yesterday, last week and so on. This simply means that what you focus on, or give your attention to, will appear in your life. You have a choice to be well or unwell.

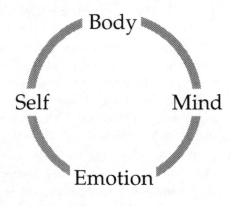

Emotions

Our emotions often get the better of us, so we are told to control or master them. To do that we use discipline, which is the most widely used form of self-control. The irony is, being yourself — or just being— does not require discipline, but willingness. The trick is to let go of using discipline to control our body, mind and emotions and use the will to nurture our whole being.

Self

The self is the seed or essence of human nature. Just as a plant knows what it is and grows naturally, so do we. Being oneself does not need discipline, control or mastery. All you need is to leave yourself alone and let go of trying to be yourself.

One of the easiest ways to apply the above is to go in the wilderness for a day or a week on your own. Take only what is absolutely necessary.

Benefits

Over past century has come the emergence of the "self-development" movement with its teachers, trainers, therapists and gurus. All this is fine but we have just as many screwed up individuals today as we did a hundred years ago, except now we have learned more about how to tinker with the mind.

Whilst I respect and admire all this effort, I believe an old solution to well-being is missing. There is a direct connection between the wilderness and well-being. For example, animals in the zoo behave and look more sickly than those in their natural habitat. In the same way if you look at people on the underground, they also appear much more sickly and paranoid than those living in the country. We are living in an artificial environment which is forcing us to behave in deranged ways. Although we can use all kinds of techniques and therapies, we cannot compensate for the absence of the wilderness. In this sense, our total well-being begins and ends by simply reconnecting ourseves to nature.

Making Changes

For Example

INSIGHT: I have become lost and confused in the world of illusion.

SOLUTION: From now on, I shall remain awake and separate illusion from reality before making choices and commitments.

ACTION: On Thursday evening I shall sit quietly and contemplate on my motivation behind the choices I make, i.e. money, property, position, education, fashion, career, colleagues, etc.

INSIGHT:

SOLUTION:

ACTION:

INSIGHT:

SOLUTION:

ACTION:

INSIGHT:

SOLUTION:

ACTION:

The Role of
H.E.L.P.

The Role of H.E.L.P.

At every stage of our evolutionary journey there has been what we call a crisis. In fact, the nature of evolution is crisis concurrent with transformation. The species which did not adapt to the crisis died. Those that did adapt had to do it so they were ready to act now — not one hundred years later! The difference between other forms of life and human beings is that we have developed our capacity to consciously project our evolution. Although we are still governed by atmospheric conditions, we have developed through the ages a capacity of consciously designing our intelligence in order to ensure our future. We worked out that the best way to secure our future was to invent it.

The difference between the current crisis and those in the past, is the real threat to our existence, to that of our children and to that of the earth. The question is, with all our scientific expertise and spiritual knowledge, why is humanity in a state of flux? Exactly what is it that is preventing us from adapting to changing circumstances and moving on? One of the major springboards in our evolutionary journey has been the advent of the written word. For example; the tablets of stone, the Qur'an, the Bible, the Gita, the Talmud and Torah, the Tibetan Book of the Dead and so on. The irony is, the written word has become the last word! Literature, rather than life, is guiding our evolutionary process. Literature, unlike life, does not constantly change with change. Unless we constantly improve and adapt the current texts used by our species, we shall remain in a state of flux. The way to escape the flux is to trace our natural evolution of consciousness and tie it to that of the structure and function of daily life. H.E.L.P. presents the information for evolution which is rooted in life, which allows us to evolve constantly. Unlike other treatises on war, peace and politics, H.E.L.P. is designed to be developed as we evolve. Indeed it is the responsibility of each new generation to improve and update the content of this book, which is the true purpose of Human Evolution and Life Procreation.

The role of H.E.L.P. is to constantly discover new tools for transformation and disseminate them to every individual, world-wide.

Human Evolution
and Life Procreation

It is often asked whether evolution applies to humans now, as to other animals. Do the laws of natural selection still apply? The answer is neither yes nor no. It's not just a matter of the survival of the fittest. For we have so profoundly altered our environment that the meaning of the word 'fittest' has changed. Fittest for what, is the question that must be asked?

Until humans arrived on the world stage, the animals that survived were those that were the fittest and were able to combat such difficulties such as climate, heat, cold, winds and rain — in whatever combination was presented. Obtaining food and warmth were the main considerations, even for the first wandering tribes of human beings. As time has gone by, gradually these elemental difficulties have been solved (at least partly) by the progress of civilisation, by trade, commerce and science, until they constitute a minor consideration in our lives. Our intelligence is now free to be diverted to our work, to learning, to science and to the conscious study of our own condition.

No longer do we fight individual battles for survival: we now depend on others to perform our part, whilst each takes a portion of what they produce and provides their own contribution to others. For example, If you think how a loaf of bread reaches you, you begin to realise how many people you depend on for it, and how interconnected we all are.

Sadly, the evolution of humanity does not deal so much with individuals anymore, except where illness and accidents are concerned. It is institutions, companies and corporations that have taken on greater importance and that authorise extensive use of the planet's resources which they have amassed in their endless greed for profit, power and control.

Modern society has introduced its own purpose into evolution. Humans work, so it is believed, for peace, happiness and the welfare of individuals. Strategic investment into our welfare and future, implies conscious evolution. There is no doubt that until now evolution has been a clumsy process — albeit efficient. Mere survival, because of chance or accidentally avoiding war, is very slow at obtaining improvement in life's handiwork. But, by the method of co-operation, our consciousness and mind have evolved. For the first time evolution has become aware of itself — like a child growing up. So that now, perhaps, we shall be able to decide what is universally desirable for humanity in the future, and work for it consciously rather than by accident. Some like to think that all the way through history there has been a vital force at work, striving for perfection, and this will still modify the changes to come. Others conceive life as struggling upward, forming ever more integrated wholes (in that a cell is a more perfect whole than a crystal).

Whatever one believes, it is through human beings, with our minds, morals and consciousness, that evolution could perhaps rise to what we would call godlike forms. Perhaps, indeed, God or *"The Kingdom of Heaven"* is the logical goal of evolution. Like alchemists, we can transform ourselves from lead to gold.

The next phase of our evolutionary journey I have termed Procreative Evolution, where those living procreatively co-operate with each other towards consciously creating our future. The best way to ensure a bright and beautiful world is for humanity to create it! I believe this process of procreative evolution is based on four basic principles which have played a critical role in the evolution of humanity.

- **The vision of the future**
- **The leadership that empowers by example**
- **Communication of the vision**
- **Co-operation in a worldwide programme for change**

To date no one has presented or implemented a neutral and practical model and method for procreative evolution which can enable each individual worldwide to participate without having to join an organisation or make a financial or material contribution. The H.E.L.P. Programme calls upon the individual's conscience, not for his or her membership. The truth is you are already a member of humanity and to join or pay for procreative evolution is a contradiction in terms. Each one of us is not a member or part of evolution, we are human evolution! The H.E.L.P. Programme is not an organisation, cult or religion, it is an educational method which presents the most common tools and methods for promoting procreative evolution. Your contribution to procreative evolution begins with discovering your personal vision for the future.

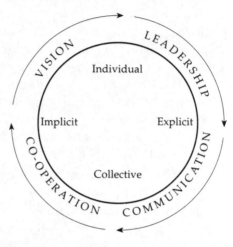

Vision

Let yourself dream for a minute, and project yourself a thousand years into the future. Imagine you have a magic wand and with it you can make anything happen. Visualise a world where miracles are commonplace and occur naturally as a result of love, peace and compassion. Imagine your country playing a helpful role in the United Nations. Narrow your vision to a local event in your community where people have enough to eat, a place to live and work for their livelihood. Look upon yourself as the wizard who has the magic skills to make this dream come true. Before you awaken from the dream ask yourself, how would you be living in a thousand years and how would it be different from now? What kind of world would it be? What would you call such a place? Imagine the way in which you could build such a world — starting from today. Do you like this dream and do you care enough to help create such a world? If you do then keep dreaming, for a dream is nothing other than a goal with a set completion date.

Leadership

As the world becomes increasingly complex, turbulent and unpredictable, there is now a need for highly committed and competent people. This applies at all levels of our society, particularly where people need the most help. In these times of crisis people look to their leaders for inspiration and direction — but do they look in vain? The majority of our leaders are position conscious and have become nestified in their ivory towers — separate from the common folk. True leaders such as Buddha, Gandhi, Jesus, Mohammad, Martin Luther King and Mother Teresa led by taking the lowest position. True leadership consists of actions which have transcended glamour and greed, becoming a function of honesty, simplicity and service.

All great leaders have these things in common: they use love, truth, humility, kindness, compassion and service to help other people. It is their ability to help fellow humans that gives them the right to be leaders. The moment we utter the words *"how can I help?"*, we take the position of service and thus become a leader. Leadership begins by learning to help oneself and then each other, our community, country and the world.

Communication

The secret of procreative evolution is a procreative humanity. The question is, how do we communicate the notion of procreative evolution to more than five billion people? We could use leaflets, letters, newspapers, books, tapes and TV but even then there is no guarantee that the idea will be accepted. The solution is simpler than the problem. The secret of communicating a message is to demonstrate the examples working in one's own life. For instance, Buddha did not launch a massive marketing campaign to spread his message. He relied on the simple truth of *"monkey see, monkey do!"* This is known as the principle of the hundredth monkey.

On an island in the Pacific, the locals practised a religious ritual where rice was used. Over a period of time the monkeys learned to wash the rice by throwing it in the water. When all the monkeys on that island could practice that 'trick', monkeys on a nearby island caught on without any communication. In the same way, messages are passed via practice within humanity. As one becomes procreative so will another and another, until we reach a critical mass when it doubles and quadruples . . . It only takes one person to make a snowball into an avalanche! We must live by example.

Co-operation

We humans are social beings. We need the help of others to survive the rigours of society. We find that tasks are easier, projects get completed in less time and the fruits of labour are multiplied when individuals co-operate. Yet, many facets of modern life effectively separate people from each other. Personal transportation, telephones and TV's separate people from face-to-face contact.

These technological trade-offs have seeded an alienation, a loneliness, a longing for belonging and a striving for identity. The media preys on this incessantly, subtly implanting these capitalist ideas and images in virtually every movie, advertisement and political broadcast.

The H.E.L.P. Programme too will use all means of communication including the media, yet the emphasis is on co-operation not coercion. With personal involvement, we are creating effective channels that best suit your needs and the needs of the community you live in. Indeed, the word 'communication' originates from 'community' and 'communion', meaning: coming together — becoming one. From communication comes co-operation which is a fancy word for helping each other. H.E.L.P. is based on the notion of co-operation — helping each other is the driving force behind procreative evolution. It results in natural networks that serve individual needs without exploitation or the use of coercion. In this sense, the notion of help (love) holds magical powers for creating a world living in peace and ease. From the moment we help each other, life becomes easier, and the more we help, the easier it becomes. Even something as simple as holding someone's hand can turn pain into a living paradise. Each act of help is like a drop which slowly and gradually sends ripples around the world.

What is the H.E.L.P. Programme?

The H.E.L.P. Programme represents humanity's endeavour to evolve and accept responsibility for itself and the earth as a whole. It attempts to link human consciousness to evolution by providing the tools and models that enable us to assume responsibility for our future. The H.E.L.P. Programme is based on what I have termed Procreative Evolution. Procreative Evolution means that as humans we are responsible for our own lives and the future. That we are creators who can create anything imaginable. Look at the word responsibility — 'response - ability' — the ability to choose one's response.

Highly procreative people recognise that responsibility. They do not blame circumstances, conditions or conditioning for their behaviour. Their responses are a result of their own conscious choice, based on vision and values, rather than their conditions which are based on external circumstances. In the words of Gandhi, *"They cannot take away our self-respect if we do not give it to them"*. In other words, what happens to us is due to our wilful consent.

What this means in reality is either you are responsible for your life, or they are. If they are, then you'd better shut up and take whatever comes your way! I admit this is very hard to accept emotionally, especially if up until now we'd thought that our problems were basically caused by sources outside ourselves, i.e. our family and friends, teachers, politicians and society in general. But, until a person can say deeply and honestly, *"I am what I am today because of the choices I made yesterday"*, that person cannot say, *"I choose otherwise"*.

It is said that a human being can fly higher than the angels or sink lower than the animals. This implies that each one of us is capable of creating our own realities.

Procreative Living

Humans are by nature procreative. If our lives are a function of conditioning or conditions, it is because we have, by conscious decision or ignorance, chosen to let those things or people control us. In making such a choice we become reactive.

Reactive people are often controlled by their physical environment. Reactive people are driven by their instincts. They react impulsively to external stimuli, be it on TV, at work, or on the street. If the weather is good they feel good, if the weather is bad then their attitude and performance goes down.

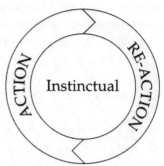

Proactive people carry their own weather with them. Whether it rains or shines makes no difference to them. The essence of a proactive person is the ability to use any adverse situation or advantage as an opportunity for growth and prosperity. Proactive people follow their intelligence, not their instincts. They have the initiative and the responsibility to make things happen. This is why a lot of powerful, rich people are proactive.

However, being proactive does not necessarily mean you are in a healthy state. Hitler and his commanders were very proactive. Proactivity is often ego driven and can result in domination. It lacks the intuitive impulse which originates from Divine Will. Turn on the news and you will see how many of our leaders in the church, state and government are proactive. They are preoccupied with the duality of profit and power, success and greatness — their ego is in control.

Procreative people are driven by intuition. Procreative people live four-dimensionally. They are intuitively guided and use their proactive freedom to do the Will of the infinite spirit. They are motivated by service which brings goodness — not greed and greatness. A truly procreative person can make things happen without position or possession, because they are propelled by the infinite force — love.

Taking the initiative to move from a reactive to a procreative lifestyle is easier than we'd like to think, for there is nothing harder than being reactive! Most human beings are well oriented towards what is truly best for them. Doing what comes naturally, very often, is what comes from within. In this respect, our lives are a reflection of the way we see things. A very common way of saying this is "what you see is what you get". This simple saying means that what you focus on will appear in your life. We create our lives by our thoughts, our words, beliefs and aspirations. What we hold in our minds becomes the reality in our lives.

What I think is what I will create.
What I say will happen to me.
What I believe is what I will become.
What I love is what I will receive.

We attract to ourselves what we have in our minds. If we have something in our lives that we don't like, we can look within and examine our thoughts about it. The transformation from reactive to proactive to procreative living is done by changing our thoughts and beliefs. Changing our negative thoughts about ourselves is a way to change our lives and to consciously create our own reality — we are the creators and we can create anything imaginable.

Procreative Living

Procreative living is a new dimension of existence in the evolution of humanity. Yet, how do we actually move from a reactive, to proactive, to a procreative way of life?

*The first step is to replace fear with faith.*It is the fear of 'lack'— 'of not having enough' — which prevents us from living procreatively. You have to understand that the earth has sustained all life-forms on its surface since the dawn of creation. It is the only planet in our solar system that sustains and supports life-forms. From the air you breathe, the sun which keeps us warm, the fruits of the trees to the water in the seas. The whole ecosystem of this planet is solely oriented towards sustaining and promoting Human Evolution and Life Procreation. Just as the Earth is procreative by nature, so are you.

The second step is to start using intuition — the key to procreative living. Living by intuition is understanding and acknowledging that the earth is "on our side". This is why new-born animals naturally feel the earth is a safe place to 'be'. Instead of trying to control nature and your lives with reasoning and intellect, let intuition guide you. At first you may occasionally have flashes of illumination or intuition, then fall back into the world of darkness. Be patient, be still and be poised to pick up your intuitive leads. Be ready to enter what Jesus called "The Kingdom".

The third stage is choice. Every day, we have the opportunity to totally transform the quality of our existence. Today you will have at least seventy thousand thoughts and yet over ninety-five percent of your behaviour may be the same as yesterday. Life is not a chance, it's a choice. You can make one choice today and forever change the way you live. If you choose to have miracles happen to you, so they shall. Expect miracles in your health, home, family and creativity. Your subconscious mind will then manifest miracles. Maybe you need a financial miracle! Choice — the metaphysical law of attraction — will activate the physical law of supply and demand. Faith, intuition and choice will bring you new life.

Which Way?

Every day, every moment, there is a fork in your life. You are at such a fork now. Now is the appointed time. Listen to your intuition and it will take you on a magical path, where miracles shall follow miracles and wonders shall never cease.

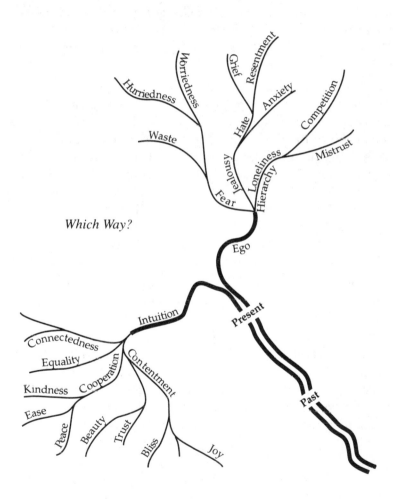

Which Way?

I was once a homeless street kid, travelling into oblivion. Being alone, there was no one to tell me what to think or do. Unknowingly, I listened to my intuition — the source of my fortune. Intuition has provided the clarity, faith and direction to overcome all manner of fears, phobias and challenges. It has awakened me. For example, at the age of fourteen my mother died and I had a choice — to stay where I was or to begin a journey of discovery. Then in my youth, I was at another crossroads where the choice was either to join a monastery or the Royal Marine Commandos. Those choices, based on intuition have brought me here . . . My life is paradise.

I have had many demonstrations of the power of intuition in my life. The most recent one was on the 1st of August '95. I was invited to spend the summer on a farm in Normandy, in France. It was a beautiful, clear evening and a polo game was in progress. On the edge of the field, a woman called Pauline was instructing Eugenie, a girl of nine, how to ride. This time as the little girl galloped past where I was sitting, I sensed fear. Soon the horse was in full gallop and I gave chase. At a distance I saw her fall. By the time I had reached her, some five seconds had elapsed and she lay motionless with her head in a distorted position. There was no breath, no pulse and checking her eyes, clearly she had gone unconscious on impact — her lungs had collapsed.

I was in a dilemma. To give her mouth to mouth, I had to move her head away from her chest, which would kill her if the spine had been severed on impact. The question was which way do I move her body and how far. Going on my intuition, I moved the head far enough to give her mouth to mouth resuscitation. Within two minutes she had started to breathe by herself. She had broken all her rib's as well as the collar bone on her left side and punctured a lung. It was a miracle that Eugenie was alive.

During this whole incident my state of being was exactly the same as I described under 'The Aim'. That of total awareness in the midst of chaos. Being itself is a precondition to intuition. The decisions made in that state of being are beyond reasoning. The Bible speaks often of "the still small voice". It is a voice which is heard by the mind.

No matter how impossible the challenge appears, through intuition you will know the solution. Intuition is faster than thought. It is direct knowing: "Before ye call I have answered". When we ask for guidance and lay aside the reasoning mind, we are tapping the universal supply of all knowledge. Everything you need to know will be revealed to you; everything you need will be given to you.

Intuition is what I call seeing with your third eye. By the third eye I do not mean an eye in the middle of the forehead. I mean foresight. Most of our decisions are made based on hindsight, i.e. the past and the present. Intuition is a metaphysical (beyond the physical) faculty which is beyond the reasoning mind. With intuition we can see outside time and space, outside of the physical reality. It enables us to make the best decisions. In a world of chaos and darkness we can find our way with intuition. Intuition is the ultimate compass by which to navigate. Let intuition be your compass and it will take you into the land of wonders.

Personal and Universal Responsibility

Whether we know it or not, each one of us has come into the world to perform our function. In fact every thought and action is another step towards completing what we have come to do. This journey from conception to death is referred to as one's destiny. The notion of destiny is often misunderstood and shrouded in mystery. For me, destiny has two sides, personal and universal — the personal destiny of my own life and the universal destiny of humanity and the whole.

At the moment of conception we enter into a body which then assumes our identity. Then we give this identity a name. Your name then becomes your truth. Personal destiny is based on personal truth — what we believe to be true for ourselves. For example, a child believes its ball belongs to it and no one else. In the same way, we are brought up to believe that all our possessions including the body belong to us. This is our personal truth and we have the responsibility to take care of what has been entrusted to us.

We take care of ourselves by eating, learning, working, buying a house, having a family, etc. In order to fulfil our personal destiny, we must focus on taking responsibility for our own needs and wants. Fulfilling personal responsibility comes from our instinctual nature and can be traced back millions of years. All animals spend the majority of their time and energy performing actions which ensure their survival. Because our survival is the most important thing, we too tend to focus on 'me' and what is mine.

Unlike animals, human beings have the capacity to comprehend a bigger picture in which they can consciously participate.

The ability to contribute consciously to the whole is the ability to fulfil one's universal responsibility. Of course all this sounds very nice in words, but what does it actually mean to embark on a journey of fulfilling one's universal destiny? Although the notion of universal responsibility sounds enormous, even impossi-

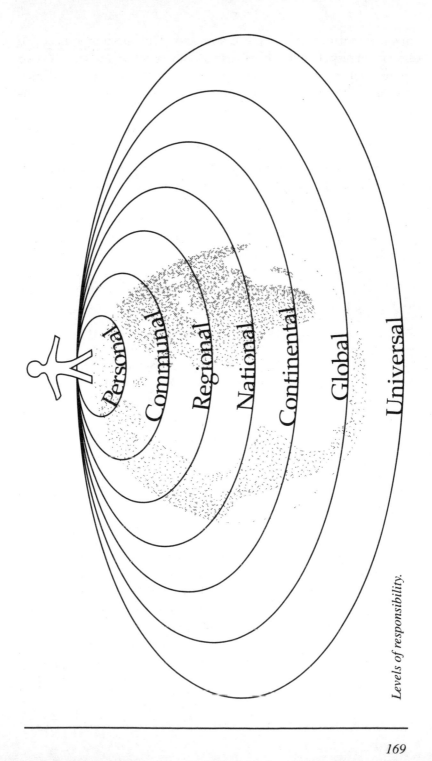

Levels of responsibility.

ble, it is in truth very simple and as easy. The question is, how can universal responsibility be as easy as taking care of ourselves? With individual responsibility, we follow our instincts; with universal responsibility, we follow our intuition. We surrender our will self-lessly to do what is necessary for the whole. *"Do not as I will, but as thou wilt."* Life gets easier the further we evolve from the animals and the more responsibility we can fulfil.

The two main reasons why we do not embark on fulfilling our universal responsibility is because we think we are alone and there-fore powerless. The following analogy may help to change that. Imagine yourself as part of the ocean. Then one day you come ashore and like a salt doll you wonder far and wide. You feel lonely and lost. Returning to the same place you re-enter the ocean and once again you become part of the whole. Intuition re-connects us to the whole. The way to put this analogy into practice is contained in the following words:

Infinite spirit guide me to do your will.

Listening to our intuition is the first step towards assuming univer-sal responsibility. The second is to act in accordance to the guidance. We often talk about being unlimited beings, but what is it that stops us from demonstrating those words and wishes? — FEAR.

There comes a time when all the thinking, meditating, praying, and preparing have been done. The one thing that is left is the ac-tual leap into the unknown — somewhat like a chick leaving the nest on its first flight. That leap is powered by the invisible force of FAITH.

A bird in the nest which refuses to fly stays nest bound. Stunted in body, courage and daring, it eventually dies in the nest. The safety of the nest is supposed to be short lived. The time has come to fly, and those who refuse to fly enter the realm of death. We can peer fearfully over the side of our personal nests and see the distance we could fall. Or we can have faith and dare to fly. Facing both the fear and the freedom, we willingly let go of the known for the unknown.

The Way Forward

The wonderful journey of H.E.L.P. began with the first humans, who instinctively used these skills in order to survive and thrive. Our ability to apply these simple skills, albeit unconsciously, speeded up our evolutionary process and raised us to the next phase in our evolutionary journey. By learning how to use these skills consciously, we can now move from instinctual evolution to conscious evolution. Conscious evolution, as we have seen is the most advanced growth process of any form of organism, organisation or being, which evolves to a more conscious and purposeful role in the universe.

Our transformation from evolution to conscious evolution can be compared to the birth of a baby. For instance, when we compare ourselves in time with the origins of life on earth, some three billion years ago, then humanity with ten million years on the earth is the equivalent of a child learning to walk. Is it any wonder that we are stumbling and making a mess of things? What humanity needs now is evolutionary guidance at this critical age. In effect, the schooling of our species to learn and grow into a happy and healthy humanity!

> *"Human history becomes*
> *more and more a race between*
> *catastrophe and education".*
>
> H.G. Wells.
> (Outline of History)

Just as we have evolved from Homo hibilis to Homo erectus, we must now evolve from Humans to Panhumans — the next phase of our evolutionary journey. However, this transformation demands that we let go of the very system which has been the driving force behind our evolution. We have reached a critical point in our evolutionary journey, where we must take a quantum leap from the 'hunter - hunted' to the 'helper - helped' system of survival.

This 'new way' of co-existence has been developing for thousands of years in isolated pockets around the world. What we need now is for each one of us to become aware of our part in a worldwide programme for communicating the means and methods of human co-operation. In doing so we add momentum to the wave of consciousness that is sweeping the planet day after day. When we reach a critical mass in the number of individuals who are participating, there will take place a quantum leap from competition to co-operation. It is up to us.

When individuals are working together
by exchanging ideas and helping each other,
then we benefit as a whole,
just as individual cells come together
to grow and form a single organism.

Further Help

Having read the book you may feel inspired and wish to connect with other like-minded people. For that purpose we have established the H.E.L.P. Programme which is conducted as follows:

- **The H.E.L.P. Seminars**
  - These seminars are for those who wish to explore further the potential and practice of the H.E.L.P. Programme.
  - They are usually conducted over a weekend and at a place near you.
  - The seminar is delivered by us. Participation: 20+; Cost: T.B.A.
  - We provide you with the materials and support for you to organise the seminar.
  - In this way each seminar promotes a sense of community and generates a continuum after the event.

- **H.E.L.P. Support Groups / Network**
  - These informal meetings are a great way to help each other improve the quality of our lives or simply to be together.
  - They can be organised by networking on the phone, by flyers for placing ads in the local shops and newspapers.
  - If you feel isolated in your area, then write to us.

- **Help us to help you**
  - This programme was launched in 1995 and is still in its early stage of development.
  - We welcome new ideas and possibilities regarding the H.E.L.P. Book, tapes and seminars.
  - We also need volunteers for the H.E.L.P. Programme.

For further information and suggestions write to:

The H.E.L.P. Programme,
PO Box 929, Wimbledon,
SW19 2AX, London, U.K.

Introducing Findhorn Press

Findhorn Press is the publishing business of the Findhorn Community which has grown around the Findhorn Foundation, co-founded in 1962 by Peter and Eileen Caddy and Dorothy Maclean. The first books originated from the early interest in Eileen's guidance over 20 years ago and Findhorn Press now publishes not only Eileen Caddy's books of guidance and inspirational material, but many other books, and it has also forged links with a number of like-minded authors and organisations.

For further information about the Findhorn Community and how to participate in its programmes please write to:

The Accommodation Secretary
Findhorn Foundation
Cluny Hill College, Forres IV36 0RD, Scotland
tel. +44 (0)1309-673655 fax +44 (0)1309 673113
e-mail reception@findhorn.org

For a complete catalogue, or for more information about Findhorn Press products, please contact :

Findhorn Press
The Park, Findhorn, Forres IV36 0TZ , Scotland
tel. +44 (0)1309-690582 fax +44 (0)1309-690036
e-mail thierry@findhorn.org
http://www.mcn.org/findhorn/press/   or
http://www.gaia.org/findhornpress

**You can order more copies of
The H.E.L.P. Book
from your local bookshop;
alternatively,
please complete the order form below,
and send directly to**

Findhorn Press Mail Order
The Park, Findhorn, Forres IV36 0TZ , Scotland
tel. +44 (0)1309-690582 fax +44 (0)1309-690036
e-mail thierry@findhorn.org

Order form

Please send me ..... copies of The H.E.L.P. Book
    at £7/US$13 each   ....
Postage & packing:
    free in the UK
    10% of order value in European Community   ....
    20% of order values in the rest of the world
Total value of order   ....

• Cheque enclosed   • Please debit my Visa/Mastercard
N° .... expiry date ..../....
Name ....
Address ....
....
....